Shortcuts to the Obvious

How to Get More Effective Advertising More Efficiently—An Insider's Guide

2nd Edition

Mel Sokotch

Table of Contents

1 Introduction, or Why *Shortcuts* is right for these times

The pioneer broadcast journalist Edward R. Murrow once said, "The obscure takes time to see, the completely apparent takes longer." Murrow was not talking about advertising; he was talking geopolitical events and why the perspective of time is needed to understand why they take place. His high hope that once the apparent is seen, it gets recorded and remembered, and helps inform a better outcome next time similar forces are gathering.

It's an important lesson with wide application, but in the advertising business, it's regularly ignored. A client of mine, Irwin Kadaner, an executive at Colgate-Palmolive, would put it this way: "I've worked with ad agencies for twenty years and it baffles me that agency people never seem to learn from their mistakes or, for that matter, their successes." He'd then rail about how we were wasting our time, and his money.

Kadaner was right then. He's more right today. There are two fundamental reasons why.

First, an ad agency's most important asset is undeniably its creative staff: Its copywriters, art directors, producers. What drives the best of them is the opportunity to do original work that breaks through the clutter. This is as it should be. But the mission has a downside. Many creative people consider advertising's rules, conventions, "lessons learned" the enemy of originality. It's this tension that's arguably an agency's greatest challenge: How to increase the odds of success without decreasing the drive to be inventive?

Second, the dilemma's getting worse. The last two decades of mergers, acquisitions, bursting bubbles have left the agency business in a lean, reactionary state. Twenty, thirty years ago the big agencies made enough money to invest in the *study time* it takes to understand what's working, and the *class time* it takes to teach the lessons. Today, it's mostly about getting the ad out on schedule.

That brings us to the basic reason for this work. With so little advertising education taking place, and with the business becoming more complex, it seemed to me that a short volume on the best lessons, and the most common mistakes, is needed and timely.

Shortcuts to the Obvious deals with the most important issues along the way to effective advertising. But the main focus is on the advertising campaign itself. That's where the real leverage is in this business. When a client buys a media schedule, the value received rarely equals the money spent. Either it's more or it's less, depending on the campaign. A great campaign turns a $20 million schedule into impact worth $30 or $40 million; a campaign that's wanting diminishes the $20 million to $15 million.

In this second edition of *Shortcuts to the Obvious*, the subject of positioning is dealt with in a much more comprehensive way. That's because I've now a much keener appreciation of the essential role effective positioning plays in the development of effective advertising. The successful brand today might have four, five agencies working on its business. They must all be on the same page, aiming at the same target, driving the same message. That's never easy. But without a clear, savvy, inspiring positioning, it's far more difficult.

As to how the lessons will be taught, the best teacher is always the best examples. *Shortcuts* will be long on the real world, short on the abstract. We'll learn from some of the best campaigns ever produced, including those for Visa, Mac, Oreo, AFLAC, Nike, American Express, Viagra, Lipitor, and Pepsi. We'll take advice from some lesser-known but no less successful campaigns, like those for Topol Toothpaste and Motel 6.

Let me also state upfront that while most of these campaigns involve multiple media, and increasingly the Internet, TV continues to be their primary medium. That's why many of the lessons taught here originate with TV advertising. Reading this, some are now taken aback, believing incorrectly the alarmist press proclaiming the demise of the TV commercial.

The hard facts suggest otherwise. As shown in the table on page 4, from 2007 to 2011, TV not only maintained its dominance, it actually grew, despite the fact that total spending is still below where it was before the Great Recession.

Take a closer look. You'll see that Internet and mobile are the fastest-growing media, while the paper/print options are dramatically off—an obvious and important cause and effect. And the reason why I've added a new chapter devoted to digital media, as solid, repeatable lessons have now been learned.

Who should read *Shortcuts*? Anyone importantly involved in the advertising development process, but especially the clients on the front line responsible for executing their brand's marketing plans. One learns early in this business

Spending by Medium ($millions)

	2007	2011 (Proj.)	%Change
Broadcast TV	47,983	44,273	–8%
Cable & Satellite TV	27,094	32,678	21%
Total TV	**75,077**	**76,951**	2%
Newspapers	51,419	26,947	–48%
Branded Entertainment	22,296	28,060	26%
Internet	18,495	25,186	36%
Broadcast & Satellite Radio	19,980	15,684	–22%
Yellow Pages	15,971	11,775	–26%
Consumer Magazines	14,451	10,371	–28%
Business-to-Business	11,267	8,261	–27%
Out-of-Home	7,966	7,812	–2%
Mobile	831	2,780	235%
Entertainment	698	1,559	123%
Total	**238,451**	**215,386**	**–10%**

Source: Veronis Suhler Stevenson Communications Industry Forecast

that they who control the advertising purse strings wield enormous influence over the advertising they get. What our clients know or don't know about the subject invariably makes a big difference.

A few words on how best to use *Shortcuts to the Obvious*. The subtitle says it all, *An insider's guide on how to get more effective advertising more efficiently.* So, when you're dealing with brand positioning or creative strategy, or approving a media schedule, or about to review a storyboard—pull *Shortcuts* down off the shelf, go to the relevant chapter, and take a minute or two to remind yourself of the several things that count most. You'll save many times that small investment and increase the odds you'll end up with advertising that's truly effective: advertising that motivates immediate action and builds strong, well-differentiated brands.

2 Successful Brands— What they are, and how to know you've got one

There's a great scene in B*arbarians at the* G*ate,* the best seller that chronicled the buyout of RJR/Nabisco in the 1980s:

> *The bankers, the venture capitalists, the lawyers are holed-up late one night debating whether to up their bid, when one player cuts to the chase with the obvious: "Oreo, Chips Ahoy, Life Savers–these are all great brands with extraordinary intrinsic value." They raised their bid, won the prize, and went on to make hundreds of millions.*

It's a great story, and the ultimate example of why a strong, well-differentiated brand is marketing's first prize. And since advertising played a disproportionate role in the creation of Nabisco's brands—as advertising does most successful brands—let's begin our journey with an exacting definition of a successful brand.

The clearest, most demanding definition ever, plus examples

On the day this paragraph was written, a Google search for "definition of a brand" yielded over thirty thousand options.

It's a popular subject. But try reading the first ten definitions—they deliver more confusion than clarity; they're all over the lot.

Let's then attempt to lift the fog with a rigorous definition—not for just any brand, but for brands considered *successful*. As the "barbarians" understood, successful brands are assets of immense value. Once built, they're hard to take down.

A successful brand is a person, place, product, or service that's:

1. **broadly recognized by a group of people with common interests;**
2. **for consistently delivering a relevant benefit or combination of benefits;**
3. **in a way that's well-differentiated from its competition.**

As we know, good definitions require no explanation; they stand on their own. But given the high importance of this one, let's take a moment to review the thinking behind its three criteria:

- The first criteria refers to the fact that successful brands always enjoy positive awareness among a high percentage of target customers. But high brand awareness is never easily achieved. It typically requires a significant media investment, plus an impactful campaign.
- The second is about the trust and confidence that's earned only after a brand's promise is consistently kept. Remember, your customer almost always has choices. Disappoint them even once, and you'll lose them.

- The third requirement is what *Shortcuts* is mostly about. Let me explain: Exclusivity is an advantage that is almost always short-lived. Most break-through products soon face close-in competition. As a result, *the way your brand presents itself soon becomes the way it differentiates itself*. And this requires a combination of experience, creativity, and the ruthlessness to make difficult choices.

Let's now bring our new definition to life with several real-world examples. And let's do that from the customer's perspective. After all, *how your customer describes your brand is the ultimate test*.

Now, when most of us are asked to describe something, we typically answer in the form of a declarative sentence. It's no different with brands. Here then are the declarative sentences that loyal customers might use to describe ten highly successful brands (with the word count for each):

1. **Dan Brown:** Writes popular novels that probe secret societies. (7)

2. **Mac:** The PC that's easier to use and more reliable. (9)

3. **Williamsburg, VA:** The place where one can experience colonial America. (8)

4. **Navy SEALs:** The elite military unit that undertakes dangerous, clandestine missions. (9)

5. **GARDASIL:** The vaccine that prevents cervical cancer in young girls. (9)

6. **Bayer:** The aspirin that protects against heart disease. (7)

7. **eBay:** The online marketplace where you can buy or sell anything. (10)

8. **Southwest Airlines:** The low-fare, no-frills airline. (6)

9. **Bono:** The world's most politically active rock star. (7)

10. **FOX:** The cable network with a conservative bent. (7)

Note that each of these sentences is very brief, none longer than ten words. This is not surprising. As we know, the fewer words, the less memory required, the easier the thought—or positioning—is to remember. This is an important theme that we'll revisit many times.

Note also that just one brand on our list faces no competition, the vaccine GARDASIL. Each of the remaining nine face direct and often vigorous competition. How, then, do these nonexclusive enterprises get so many people describing them in such differentiated terms? The answer begins with effective positioning, the important subject of chapter three.

Reality Check

First, write down the sentence you'd want your customer to play back when asked to describe your brand. Make sure it's no more than ten words. Next, ask your most loyal customers to describe your brand in ten words or less. This can be done at minimal cost via the do-it-yourself online research services. If the research finds that your words match those of your customers', then your campaign is working well. But if they don't match, if they're clearly different, then either your positioning needs adjusting or your communications program needs fixing.

3 Positioning—First step, guiding light, ruthless taskmaster

The most efficient way to build a successful brand is to make sure every aspect of the enterprise is guided rigorously by an inspired and savvy *positioning statement*.

But before we get to definitions and process, here's an instructive story from Chip and Dan Heath's terrific book, *Made to Stick*. The word *positioning* is never mentioned, but this story describes perfectly what positioning is all about:

> *Herb Kelleher, long-time CEO of Southwest Airlines, tells a friend "I can teach you the secret to running the airline in 30 seconds. This is it: We are THE low-fare airline. Once you understand that fact, you can make any decision about this company's future as well as I can."*
>
> *"Here's an example," he said. "Tracy from marketing comes into your office. She says her surveys indicate that passengers might enjoy a light entrée on the Houston to Vegas flight. All we offer is peanuts, and she thinks a nice chicken Caesar salad would be popular. What do you say?"*
>
> *The person stammered for a moment, so Kelleher responded: "You say, 'Tracy, will adding that chicken Caesar salad make us THE low-fare airline from Houston to*

*Vegas? Because if it doesn't help us become the unchal-
lenged low-fare airline, we're not serving any damn
chicken salad.'"*

Whether Southwest actually has a formal positioning statement, I don't know, but there can be no doubt this brand is rigorously guided by the principles of classic positioning.

The positioning statement: definition, content, format

Let's begin by clearing up the difference between *positioning* and *positioning statement*. They're often used interchangeably, but there's an important difference.

- **Positioning** *is* the couple of words you want your customers thinking when they think about your brand. The best way to express positioning is with a short declarative sentence. The ten we reviewed in the last chapter are great examples. (We'll come back to positioning later, after we've dealt with the *positioning statement* that informs it...)
- The ***positioning statement*** is a tight, exacting, complex sentence that sums up a brand's most basic reasons for being. The best tell a short story that compels action, differentiates from competition, *and is brief enough to be readily understood by everyone who touches the brand.* Needless to say, this is a sentence on which much rides.

The most effective positioning statements address five basic issues:

1. **Who, specifically, is brand's target customer?**
2. **What animating customer issue does the brand address?**
3. **In what category does the brand compete?**
4. **What is the brand's compelling promise?**
5. **What is the reason-to-believe the promise will be kept?**

Getting the answers right is deceptively hard, and then putting them into a one-sentence story can be even harder.

Here are six positioning statements, each *deconstructed* from the real-world communications of a well-defined brand:

- For middle-aged men at high risk of heart disease, **Lipitor** is the cholesterol-reducing medicine clinically proven effective at preventing heart attack and stroke. (23)

- For young adults passionate about living a healthy life, **Kashi** is the line of good-tasting all-natural foods, each made from a special recipe based on "7 whole grains." (29)

- For local travelers focused on price, **Southwest** is the airline with consistently low prices because everyone at SW works at keeping costs low and value high. (27)

- For young urban professionals who rent cars but want to avoid the hassle, **Zipcar** subscription service is the more convenient way to drive because its cars are available by the hour, by the day, in your neighborhood. (32)

- For patriotic young men looking for adventure, **Navy SEALs** is the elite military unit that provides uniquely challenging experiences with missions that are hazardous, clandestine, critical to the nation's security. (31)

- For PC users in need of new equipment, **Mac** is easier to use and more reliable because it's the only PC with hardware and software designed exclusively for each other. (31)

A couple of observations:

Note the specificity of the first phrase, the one that identifies the customer target and their animating issue. Getting this right is hard, sometimes agonizingly so. After all, the size of your business relates directly to the size of your target. *It must be big enough to make a difference, but not so big that it forces the rest of the statement into common denominators.*

- By aiming at "local travelers focused on price" rather than "anyone traveling by air," **Southwest** aimed smaller and built a big, profitable business.
- That **Mac** targeted "PC users in need of new equipment" as opposed to "anyone in the market for a PC" is what gave Mac's great campaign its sharp edge (the cool Mac guy versus the PC nerd).

Note also that the five points need not appear in a specific order; it's much more important that the sentence read well.

- In the **Lipitor** statement, for example, the reason-to-believe the promise comes before the promise (*clinically proven effective at preventing...*)
- And **Kashi** combines both promise and category in one pithy phrase (*good-tasting all-natural foods*).

The point is this: don't obsess over order; get the five key points into a clear, logical sentence. The better the sentence, the easier it is to understand, the more readily it will be accepted and applied by the many who help build your brand.

But wait, shouldn't a positioning statement include an emotional payoff?

Some do. A sixth issue is added that goes something like: What is the brand's emotional payoff? or What's the end-end benefit? The problem here is that these emotional payoffs are always and painfully obvious—and rarely differentiating. For example:

+ Southwest might have added: "...so you can feel satisfied you got a good deal."
+ Zipcar might have added: "...so you can save money for things you really love."
+ Lipitor might have added: "...so you can feel confident you're doing all you can to prevent heart disease."

Does emotion play an important role in brand communications? Absolutely! But its expression is best left to your creative partners, with their special insight into how people feel about things. Your positioning statement should focus your organization on the few issues that define and differentiate your brand. If you do that well, the "end-end benefit" will take care of itself.

The most effective way to build an effective positioning statement

There are several ways to get this done, and at varying cost. Call in a big-name consulting firm and it might cost $2 million. Call in a big-name ad agency and it might cost five, seven hundred thousand.

But positioning is too fundamental and important an issue to be left to a third party, no matter how skillful. Think about it, the positioning statement is not just a short-form description of your business; it's how you want your organization to behave. And it informs how you want your customers to think about your brand.

Positioning is a job best handled internally, and by the senior people most responsible for your brand's success. Here accordingly is an effective way to get it done: a six-step process that any organization can work with, and enjoy. It's practical, collaborative, rigorous, and efficient.

1. Enlist six or seven senior people from various disciplines who know your product or service very well: The founder or inventor, if available. Someone from the tech or R & D end; a marketing person or two; a top sales person; a seasoned agency executive; a market researcher who's spent quality time with target customers; plus someone with experience writing positioning statements. Here's where a consultant might help.

2. Give them each our five questions, plus several real-world examples, like the ones we just reviewed. Include deconstructed positioning statements from the brand's close-in competition. Hand out a homework assignment: Instruct each participant

to answer our five key questions. Give the group two weeks to complete the assignment.

3. Then get them in a conference room, a comfortable one, preferably off-campus. Have each participant present his or her recommended statement. Debate the options, but always measure them against the competitive benchmark. And remember, the best are short and specific.

4. You'll probably end up with several good options. How then to choose? The most objective way is with a quantitative "concept test." The finalists are put into "concepts," where the five points are rewritten into a paragraph. Here, for example, are three concepts that a team of Mac executives could have conceivably come up with. The first two differ only in reason-to-believe; the third targets a different audience:

   a. If you're a PC user who's decided to get new equipment, consider switching to a Mac. Mac is not only easier to use, it's also more reliable. Why? *Because unlike other PCs, Mac software and hardware are designed exclusively for each other.*

   b. If you're a PC user who's decided to get new equipment, consider switching to a Mac. Mac is not only easier to use, it's also more reliable. *That's why, year after year, Mac is top-rated for customer satisfaction.*

   c. *If you're a PC user determined to minimize virus attacks, consider switching to a Mac.* The odds of a Mac getting attacked are virtually nil. That's because Macs, unlike other PCs, are designed with built-in defenses nearly impossible to penetrate.

The form these positioning concepts take can vary: they're often typed paragraphs, like these Mac examples; if the product is a food or vacation destination, they might include a visual; or they can be delivered by an actor talking to camera in a low-cost video.

5. Next, quantitative testing. This is no place for the soft, often misleading results of a couple of focus groups. (See "Hazards to Avoid," on the next page.)

   As to who executes a "quant" test, the big research houses—like ARS, Ipsos-ASI, Millward-Brown, Nielsen/BASES—do a good job. They have extensive experience, standard questionnaires, norms to compare against, *and they're expensive.*

   But if you're working with savvy research people, the online do-it-yourself services can be just as reliable *at a cost that can run 75 percent less!* The key to these DYI options is an effective questionnaire. This means questions that gauge "interest" as well as "uniqueness," plus open-ended questions to get at what was motivating in the concept, what was problematic, what was believable, what was confusing.

   What about norms or benchmarks? The best benchmarks are your real-world competitors. Positioning research should always include a deconstructed concept from a direct competitor or two. This is what your customers will benchmark you against. You should too!

6. How to evaluate the research results? Here are three scenarios:

   a. If one of the concepts scores significantly better than the alternatives and better than the benchmarks, then it's easy: This is your choice.

b. If the results are encouraging, but there are no big differences, then a careful reading of the verbatim answers to the open-ended questions becomes very important. If the verbatims for one concept are more robust, more passionate, then that's a good sign.

c. But if none of your concepts beat your competition, this raises two difficult questions. Are your concepts poorly constructed? or Is there a fundamental issue with your business proposition? Either way, serious rethinking is necessary.

Hazards to Avoid

Focus group research is sometimes helpful, sometimes misleading, and always expensive. Conduct nine groups, six people per group, in three cities, and the cost can run $150,000. That's about $3,000 per participant. But there's always one person who talks too much, and one who says nothing. That makes it $4,000 per "representative" customer. And let's not forget that most focus group participants are "professional" focus group participants. So, does anyone in their right mind think they're getting objective feedback, let alone good value, from a focus group? When it comes to positioning, quantitative research will help you make a better decision, at a lower cost.

How to use the positioning statement

The Southwest story says it all: Your brand's positioning statement should be learned and embraced by everyone who touches your brand, and then applied every day—and not just by marketing people and their ad agencies, but also by the people in sales, finance, personnel, R&D, manufacturing, and all the rest. They too have a vested interest in your brand's success. Here are several painless suggestions on how to help get them all on board:

1. Make sure everyone in your extended organization is reminded regularly that everything they do is ultimately in service of the brand's positioning.

2. Make sure that all new people assigned to your brand are taught its positioning statement on DAY ONE of their tenure.

3. Make sure every brand-specific recommendation is evaluated, at least in part, based on its likelihood of strengthening your brand's positioning.

4. Make sure to confirm regularly that your best customers describe your brand with language that reflects your positioning. (See "Reality Check" in the previous chapter for an efficient way to get this done.)

5. Finally, make "strengthening your brand's positioning" an important criterion in the annual evaluation of everyone with direct responsibility for management of your brand.

How to get the "positioning" out of the positioning statement

At the top of this chapter we reviewed the difference between *positioning statement* and *positioning*. The *positioning statement* informs how you want your organization to carry out their mission; the *positioning* is how you want your customer to think about your brand.

Here is the key point: Positioning statements are necessarily 30 to 35 words. That's brief enough for any organization to learn, but too many words for most consumers to remember.

It's therefore important to determine which phrases or ideas within the positioning statement you would want your customers to play back when they describe your brand.

Let's see how three well-differentiated brands answer this question:

- **Kashi** focuses its communications on its *reason-to-believe*. While most natural foods promise good taste, and many include whole grains, none claim that every product in its line contains "7 whole grains." Kashi's positioning could therefore be written as follows:

Every Kashi product is made with "7 whole grains."(9)

- **Lipitor** focuses on its target, *high-risk men*. With its efficacy claims no longer exclusive, this big brand now competes by talking specifically—and for the moment, exclusively—to a limited segment of the elevated-cholesterol population. Lipitor's deconstructed positioning:

Lipitor: The statin for men at high risk of heart disease. (10)

- But **Mac** focuses its communications squarely on its *benefit*. If you can deliver a superior benefit like "easier/more reliable,"get out of the way and drive it home:

Mac: The PC that's easier to use and more reliable. (9)

To sum up, the part of your brand's positioning statement on which your communications program should focus *is the part that's most differentiating.*

How to use your brand's positioning

First, how *not* to use its positioning: Don't judge your ad campaign by whether or not it delivers your positioning's exact words. The talented and creative people at your agency should be able to find language or metaphors or pictures that deliver your positioning with more impact.

On the other hand, make sure there's no daylight between your advertising's net takeaway and your brand's positioning.

Consider, again, Mac's great side-by-side campaign, the one featuring the cool Mac guy versus the PC nerd. Some of these commercials focused on Mac being "easier of use," others focused on "more reliable," but the campaign's net takeaway was clearly and emphatically that "Mac is easier to use and more reliable than all the look-alike PCs."

How to make sure your communications program delivers your positioning in a way that gets your customer embracing it, and playing it back? There are many ways, but the most important way is to make sure that *delivering your brand's positioning* is a goal clearly articulated in the creative brief that informs advertising development...

4 The Creative Brief— Seven questions, and how to answer them well

There's no guarantee that a shrewd, well-written creative brief will lead all the way to effective advertising, but without one, getting there is next to impossible.

The creative brief serves two purposes: First, it's the direction the agency's copywriters and art directors follow to conduct their "creative exploratory"; and second, it's the checklist against which clients evaluate the campaigns the agency recommends.

But what's essential to understand is this: When the assignment is handed over to the creative team, they go back to their workspaces by themselves with nothing more than the creative brief to guide them. Over the next several weeks, they'll refer back to it time and again.

If the creative brief is a good one, and the creative team talented, they'll return with ideas that stand a good chance of leading to effective advertising. But if the creative brief is ill conceived or poorly written, the journey will be long, hard, and expensive. When a CMO reviews a campaign exploratory and says, "I didn't realize this is where the brief would take us," it hurts and it costs, in dollars and enthusiasm.

Creative briefs come in all manner of sizes and shapes, but the best of them provide pithy, thoughtful answers to seven fundamental questions:

1. What is the goal of this advertising?
2. Who is the target customer?
3. Which are the primary competitors?
4. What fact or insight best sets up the promise?
5. What promise best motivates the target customer?
6. What makes the promise believable?
7. What are the campaign mandatories?

Answering these questions well takes insight into what motivates consumers as well as to what inspires copywriters and art directors. What follows is guidance on how each question should be approached together with model answers deconstructed from a wide range of successful campaigns.

1. What is the goal of this advertising?

This question should always be answered by identifying what we expect to happen when the ad meets up with its target. The most effective advertising always causes two things to happen:

- First, the advertising inspires the target customer to take some specific action: It could be to buy a line extension, sign-up for a new service, ask the doctor about an Rx medicine, visit a website, switch from competitive brand.
- Second, the advertising strengthens the brand's positioning by reiterating the couple of thoughts you want your target customer thinking when they think about your brand.

The best "advertising goal" statements can be written in just one sentence, as these seven examples demonstrate well:

◆ Mac

To encourage PC users to consider Mac the next time they upgrade, while reinforcing the notion that Mac is more reliable and easier to use than PC.

◆ Oreo

To cause moms of snack-loving families to stock Oreo among the cookie brands in their pantry and, at the same time, remind them that Oreo is the only cookie one can *twist, lick, dunk.*

◆ Southwest Airlines

To cause short-distance travelers to choose Southwest and remind them SW is THE no-frills, low-fare airline.

◆ Navy SEALs

To attract qualified recruits and to make clear that the SEALs' mission is challenging and critically important to the nation's welfare.

◆ Kashi

To get natural-food devotees to try Kashi while pointing up that it's always made with "7 whole grains."

◆ Lipitor

To encourage men with high cholesterol to ask about Lipitor, the statin that protects against stroke and heart attack.

♦ *Tide Stain Release*

To convince big-family moms to add new Tide Stain Release to their wash, because it removes even tough stains the first time.

Hazards to Avoid
_____

This question is often wrongly answered with statements about business goals, share-of-market objectives, or awareness targets. Information like this adds little to a creative brief. Remember, the best advertising does two things well: motivates action and builds brand equity. That's all, but that's a lot, and it's worth repeating.

---

2. Who is the target customer?

Assume the obvious: that the creative team will want to feature the target customer in their campaigns. What then are the most defining characteristics of his or her life? Include several hard facts, like: age, income, education, family size; as well as a qualitative descriptor or two, like: early adopter, financially anxious, obsessive about health, watches FOX news, intimidated by technology, cares about environment, pressed for time. An effective description can be written with just a couple of sentences. Here are four examples:

♦ *Mac*

Anyone with a PC who's ready for new equipment. Their PC has become an essential part of their daily life, both business and personal. Some are serious techies; many are not sophisticated at all. They have style; they're individualistic; and they value simplicity.

◆ Zipcar

Young urban professionals. Their lives are busy and hectic. They're always pressed for time. They don't own a car. They take cabs or public transportation to work. But they get away every couple of weekends, and they typically rent a car from one of the name providers.

◆ Viagra

Men in their fifties, sixties, seventies. They're married. They've enjoyed good sex lives. But in recent years they've had difficulty getting or keeping an erection. The reason might be a health condition, like a prostrate operation or heart disease. Or it might just have happened gradually.

◆ Kashi

Young adults who are active, involved, well educated. They care passionately about the environment. They're more likely to drive a hybrid car. They only buy energy-efficient appliances. They work at eating only organic and/or natural foods. And they'll even pay 10 to 15 percent more for it.

Hazards to Avoid

Abe Lincoln's advice about the impossibility of "satisfying all of the people, all of the time" is worth remembering here. Effective targeting means making choices, sometimes difficult choices, and that means limiting your audience. But if you do a good job with a discrete group and turn them into true believers, the rest will take care of itself.

---

3. Which are the primary competitors?

Oscar Wilde once said, "A man can't be too careful in the choice of his enemies." The same can be said about marketing. Determining who or what you're competing with, and how directly to compete, are important and subtle issues.

- **Visa** initially focused on American Express, recognizing that if it compared favorably to the "gold standard," it would compare even more favorably to MasterCard.
- **Kindle** first took aim at traditional books, but now competes against the many imitators it quickly spawned, including Apple's iPad.
- **Mac** is no longer creating a market, it now positions itself as a better alternative to the whole class of look-alike PCs.
- **Chunky Soup** suggests that it's a better meal than a frozen dinner, a category much larger than ready-to-heat soups.
- **Zipcar** competes with the established rent-a-car companies: Hertz, Avis, Enterprise, Budget, and the rest.
- **Levitra** positions itself against Viagra and Cialis, neither of which claims efficacy among men with co-morbid conditions.

Hazards to Avoid

When Yamamoto attacked Pearl Harbor he said, "I fear we may have awakened a sleeping giant." He was right, and paid dearly. If you consider a direct comparison, think through carefully how the competitor might respond, and then make a clear-eyed decision.

4. What fact or insight best sets up the promise?

Good advertising always presents a solution to an animating customer issue. It might be an everyday problem, or an unaddressed emotional issue, or a startling fact.

◆ Mac

The PC experience of target customers has been less than ideal: too often, their equipment needs troubleshooting, or it's been virus-attacked, or the service they get is inconsistent.

◆ Viagra

While the onset of ED has taken a toll on their self-image as well as their relationships, many men are still reluctant to talk about the problem with their doctors.

◆ Zipcar

Owning a car in a big city can be exorbitantly expensive. And renting one from the big-name providers can be a time-consuming hassle.

◆ Lipitor

Many patients believe that all cholesterol-reducing medicines are the same. What they don't know is that some medicines are proven to reduce the risk of a cardiovascular event, while others are not.

◆ Tide Stain Release

When active kids get tough stains on their clothes, *that's expected*. When it takes multiple washings to get these stains out, *that's frustrating*.

◆ Geek Squad

For people highly dependent on their technology, nothing creates more anxiety than a glitch or virus they can't fix quickly.

5. What promise best motivates the target customer?

The best advertising makes a promise to the customer: *Buy this product and get this benefit*. The benefit must be one that satisfies an important need or want. It must also be one that the competition cannot promise, *or is not promising*. This second part of the equation is as important as the first. Advertising that makes a me-too claim, no matter how well executed, never builds a strong, differentiated brand.

Here are several brand promises that are well-differentiated and well-received:

◆ Mac

There's no PC easier to use or more reliable than Mac.

◆ Cheer

Cheer protects the color of your clothes wash after wash after wash.

◆ Zyrtec

Only Zyrtec is FDA-approved to treat both indoor and outdoor allergies.

◆ Lipitor

Lipitor helps protect high-risk men from heart attack and stroke.

◆ *Tide Stain Release*

Tide Stain Release gets even tough stains out *the first time.*

◆ *Geek Squad*

Geek Squad is available 24/7 to fix the common problems that invariably come with personal technology.

Hazards to Avoid

Become skeptical whenever the discussion turns to *higher-order benefits.* Don't trust a technique called the "benefit ladder." The only good that comes from this exercise is the recognition that the higher up you go, the less specific things get. "SlimFast helps you lose weight in just one week." That *ladders up* to, "You'll feel better about yourself, and others will too." The same higher-order benefits could be credited to a teeth-whitening toothpaste, a new cashmere sweater, or a time-release antiperspirant.

---

6. What makes the promise believable?

This might well be the creative brief's most important question, especially since so much advertising is so hard to believe. Turn on your TV and you'll soon meet someone promising better abs, a smoother golf swing, or an improved memory. It's this crowd that your ad sometimes runs with, so special care must be taken to make a credible presentation. There are a number of techniques proven to work well:

- **Comparative Demonstrations:** For years, Cheer demonstrated it protects the color of clothes better than "another leading brand," and built a strong, unassailable business. When Visa showed that

Amex was not accepted at places like the Kentucky Derby or Bob's Lobster House, you figured you better have a Visa card in your wallet as well. Perhaps the best comparative campaign ever was the "Pepsi Challenge" where we watched Coke loyalists actually prefer Pepsi. It worked so well it caused Coke to change (temporarily) its decades-old formula.

- **Unique Facts:** In a tough fight against cheaper private labels, Chips Ahoy justified its higher price by claiming a "1,000 chocolate chips in every bag." Rolaids proved its curative powers with a fact too extraordinary not to be believed: Each tablet "neutralizes 47 times its weight in excess stomach acid." Fosamax announced that 1 of 2 women past 60 get osteoporosis, encouraged them to get a bone density test.

- **Survey Research:** Tylenol established its safety and efficacy because "more hospitals use Tylenol." Saab adds legitimacy with the fact that, "Most people who test-drive a Saab end up buying one." Lipitor proclaims it's the number-one prescribed medicine for lowering high cholesterol and benefits from the implication it must work well.

- **Third-Party Endorsements:** When the American Heart Association says that Cheerios, together with a sensible diet, helps lower cholesterol, the claim is taken seriously. When the FDA indicates that a new Rx medicine is safe and effective, we trust that it is. But when Snickers claims to be the official snack of the NYC Marathon, most of us know they bought the endorsement.

- **Special Ingredients:** Folgers Coffee tastes great because its beans are "mountain grown" (fact is, most coffee beans grow on mountains, but Folgers' made the fact its own). KFC sold lots of chicken because only the Colonel's special recipe contains "11 herbs and spices." Visine Eye Drops convinced millions it effectively "gets the red out" because it contains an active ingredient called Tetrahydrozoline, a word so scientific sounding, it immediately bestowed confidence.

- **Celebrity Endorsements:** Back in the late '70s, Nike was losing share and in real trouble. Then John McEnroe put on a pair of Nike's and won his first U.S. Open. The event turned Nike around. (They've now got a building named McEnroe.) In the early '90s, Michael Jordan endorsed Rayovac Batteries, but he accomplished nothing. No one believed him. Why would they? In the late '90s Bob Dole talked with candor and sensitivity about ED after prostate cancer, and paved the way for Viagra and the others. Celebrities can be highly effective, but only when their expertise, or their experience, is relevant.

- **Seeing is Believing:** Some promises don't need hard-fact support. When a bowl of hearty soap or a Thanksgiving turkey is photographed so well your mouth waters, that's validation enough. When the Jeep drives up and over the mountain, we assume it can handle the driveway after a snow flurry.

Hazards to Avoid

Some clients think about an ad they way they do a sales presentation, where the audience is "captured" and many support points can be made. Advertising is different. The audience does not stay put. Hence, the best ads support their promises with one good point or one good picture. Resist fiercely all the good "secondary" points that can be made. The whole will be less than the sum of its parts.

7. What are the campaign mandatories?

This final question presumes that every campaign has at least some nonnegotiable requirements that must be in every ad. Several examples:

- **Oreo** commercials must always feature a kid twisting, licking, dunking the cookie.
- All **United Airlines** commercials must use the George Gershwin classic *Rhapsody In Blue*.
- All print ads for Rx meds must "balance" benefits with warnings, and must be followed by a "brief summary" of the med's full prescribing information.
- All **Tide Stain Release** commercials must feature a before-and-after demonstration.
- All **Kashi** ads must feature Kashi employees and end with the line "7 whole grains on a mission."
- All **Aqua Fresh Toothpaste** ads must include, in a conspicuous way, an aqua-colored item. (I'm not making this up. It's true. I worked on the account.)

****

There you have model answers to the seven questions that an effective creative brief would contain. But before leaving the subject, three additional issues need addressing: How to answer the question when there are several good options? Who writes the Creative Brief? Who approves the Creative Brief?

How to get the best answers when the choices are multiple?

There are times when several very good answers are available. This is especially true for the questions on insight,

promise, and support. Choosing the best answer can sometimes be tricky. Consider, for example, the difficulty in deciding among these options:

- Which "target insight" should Mac address: that
  some PC users think that a Mac is too expensive or
  that others feel apprehensive about learning a new
  operating system?
- Should a new flu vaccine "promise" that it will "prevent lost days of work" or that it "eases the flu's se-
  vere aches and pains"?
- Is the best "support" for Visa's "everywhere"
  promise the fact that "it's honored at 99 percent of
  all credit-taking establishments" or that it's "accepted in places where Amex isn't"?

Good choices all, but how to choose? If you and your agency
partners believe one to be the best, it probably is. But without solid consensus, it's best to ask the customer, and the
best way to do that is by testing strategic concept statements, like the concepts we reviewed in the last chapter.
This is simply a short paragraph that opens with the "setup
fact or insight" followed by the "promise" and then the
"support"—much the way an ad might.

Here's how works: Let's assume we've got two very good
facts to support Visa's "everywhere" claim. How do we determine which is best? First, write two concept statements,
keeping the "insight" and "promise" exactly the same, but
varying the "support" facts. For example:

Visa's accepted where Amex isn't.

Discovering that a shop or restaurant does not honor your
credit card can be an unexpected hassle, and a very good
reason to get yourself a Visa credit card. There's no more

convenient credit card available than Visa. *In fact, Visa is accepted at thousands of establishments that don't take American Express.*

Visa's accepted virtually everywhere.

Discovering that a shop or restaurant does not honor your credit card can be an unexpected hassle, and a very good reason to get a Visa Credit Card. There's no more convenient credit card available than Visa. *In fact, Visa is accepted at 99 percent of all establishments that take credit.*

Next, get competitive cardholders to read the two concept statements, and have them tell us which is most persuasive. The most persuasive concept must therefore be based on the more persuasive support point—and so that's the one to include in your brand's creative brief.

Who should write the creative brief?

The best creative brief writer understands what motivates target customers, knows what inspires creative teams, and is an accomplished writer, as well. Who is this person? These days creative briefs are typically written by the agency Strategic Planner*. But there's no hard and fast rule. A savvy account person or a strategic copywriter can certainly do the job. Some clients insist on writing the creative strategy themselves, and some are very good at it.

*This title is misleading, as the function has nothing to do with planning. Since clarity is a hallmark of good advertising, one has to wonder why strategic planners don't clarify their title.

Who should approve it?

No matter who writes it, the creative brief must be approved by two key people: the account's senior creative director and the client who makes the final decision.

It makes little sense to tell a creative team to write against this or that creative brief without the team leader embracing the direction. This should be obvious.

What should also be obvious is that the final decision maker—and this means the client who says "Yes, ship this campaign," or "No, don't ship"—should sign-off on the brief, as well.

5 Creative Exploratory— What to look for, what risks to take

Mario Andretti once said, "If everything seems under control, you're just not going fast enough." He was talking, of course, about Formula One racing, not about advertising. But there are similarities. The Formula One driver who pushes the envelope sometimes wins, sometimes gets killed. The advertising campaign that pushes the edge sometimes breaks through, sometimes gets a bad test score.

The point is, the creative exploratory is a good time to take calculated risks. The rewards can be great, and the downside minimal, if you're disciplined about getting your customer's reaction before spending serious money.

Here's how to handle an initial creative presentation.

Before the work is presented

Two things should always happen before new creative work is presented. First, the creative strategy should be reviewed, especially the target insight, the promise, the reason-why support. Next—and this is obvious, but it happens with remarkable infrequency—the competition's advertising should be reviewed as well. Remember, effective advertising differentiates, strategically *and* executionally. Make sure what you're about to review does too.

W*hen* the work is presented

Expect to evaluate at least three original campaigns, but not more than six. Fewer than three is not a true exploratory; more than six is too much to take in—the best ideas won't get the attention they deserve.

The best creative teams present the *campaign idea* before they present the campaign. This might be done with a few sentences presented together with a key visual on a board. If the core idea is a good one, you'll know it right away. If it appears otherwise, hold final judgment until you see the work—the work sometimes does a better job of speaking for itself. Here are five "previews" that would have given the client a good understanding of the campaigns that followed:

Oreo—key visual & statement
Two kids "competing" with each other over who gets to twist open the Oreo and lick the cream side.

Mac—key visual & statement
Two thirty something guys—one cool, the other nerdy, representing Mac and PC—debate the differences between the two units.

Cheer—key visual & statement

A "continuing character" conducts side-by-side demonstrations that prove Cheer preserves color better than "another leading brand" wash after wash.

AFLAC—key visual & statement

Each spot features a duck quacking "AFLAC" while a couple of oblivious men talk about their insurance needs.

Lipitor—key visual & statement

Boomer-aged men who've suffered a recent heart attack talking about their experience and how they now trust Lipitor prevent a future attack.

The creative team then presents the full campaign, typically in storyboard form for TV; comps for print ads, banner ads or direct mail; scripts for radio. If the primary medium is TV, this is where the initial discussion should focus. Here is some guidance:

Your first impression is of singular importance. Your customers often make up their minds based on first impression, so yours should carry disproportionate weight. But choosing a campaign is a decision too important to make on first impression alone; careful analysis is called for. Suggestion: If the 5 questions below can be answered in the affirmative, then the campaign before you becomes a candidate for further evaluation.

1. Does the campaign faithfully execute the strategy?

2. Is the story line relevant, easy to follow, inherently interesting?

3. Does it differentiate the brand in message, look, and feel?

4. Does the campaign translate well to the other media?

5. Can the core idea "pool out" at least ten times?

What to do *next*

Ask questions, but attempt to keep them related to the strategy and core idea. Don't get bogged down on details. There's plenty of time to get them right.

If you like a campaign, say so with enthusiasm. If you don't, don't sugarcoat. It never does anyone any good.

Get the agency's specific recommendation. Ask the top creative person in the room which campaign to produce if advertising had to be launched on judgment alone.

If two or three campaigns on the table meet the five criteria, then "rough produce" and test them. (More about rough production later.) Make sure to include one or two campaigns like none you've ever seen. As Andretti suggests, *winning takes risk*, and this is the one time when risk can be taken without getting burned.

If, however, there's no campaign worthy of testing, or there's just one, then either the agency hasn't done its job, or maybe the strategy was flawed. A tough spot to be in, and some hard calls have to be made.

6 How to pre-test advertising, without getting burned

A Senior Vice President from one of the large research services presented test results at the agency and anxiously opened up with the comment that she knew we considered her one of the "evildoers." This is why most advertising research is presented on client turf, where the audience tends to be more civil and attentive.

But the truth is, most of the time, the research services provide good, actionable information about how customers will react to your ad. Every so often, however, their findings make no sense, or they'll be contradictory, or even flat-out wrong. Remember, we're dealing here with statistics and probability, not with absolute certainty.

> In 1948, some very sophisticated statisticians ignominiously projected Thomas Dewey, not Harry Truman, the election winner. The statistical methodologies were duly tightened up. But in 2000, it happened again, when the TV networks, based on "reliable exit polling," initially projected Al Gore the winner.

All that said, launching an expensive advertising campaign without pre-testing it makes little sense. Neither does putting blind faith into statistics and probability. Some judgment is always required.

Here then are three lessons on getting the most reliable advertising research and making the most informed advertising judgments:

1) the test ad must be representative of the final ad;
2) the research methodology must approximate the real world;
3) the resulting metrics should never be taken at face value.

Let's examine each:

1. How to produce test ads that represent finished ads

The lion's share of advertising research money goes to testing TV commercials. Print ads, radio commercials, out-of-home, Internet banners rarely get pre-tested. If TV is the campaign's lead medium, and the TV commercial tests well, it's reasonable to assume that campaign ads in other media will also test well.

On those few occasions when a print or radio ad or banner is tested, the production is easy and the cost low, often no more than several thousand dollars. Producing a representative TV commercial is another matter—it's more complex and costly, sometimes as high as $50,000. But it's an investment worth making. The research that yields a "false positive" or "false negative" because the stimulus is flawed can lead to mistakes far more costly than $50,000. Special care must be taken to produce test commercials that are reasonable facsimiles. Several production techniques are available, some better than others.

- **Live-a-matics**—These are "real" commercials shot by skeletal crews using low-cost methods like "green screen," where we first shoot actors against a green background, then later, in the editing room, add the "environment." This is a terrific technique as the test commercial is a close-in representation of the full-up commercial, which means high confidence in the research results.

- **Rip-o-matics**—Segments of other commercials are "ripped off" (actually bought from an image library), then edited together with a sound track. This technique can be effective if the right combination of similar images is available.

- **Animatics**—Artist-illustrated frames, often with crude movement, plus a sound track. The technique is popular because it's easy and inexpensive, and some research firms—but not all—claim they find animatics to be as predictive as finished commercials. But an animatic is basically a cartoon, and cartoons are not at all like air-quality commercials, unless of course they're cartoons. Animatics should be used as a last resort if, and only if, none of the more representative techniques is feasible or affordable.

- **Photo-matics**—Instead of an artist's illustrations, actual photographs are used. Photo-matics can be more representative than animatics, but can get expensive if stock photography is not available and original photography must be shot.

None of these techniques is perfect, but the more real world the test stimuli, the more predictable the research results—an important and obvious lesson too often ignored.

Hazards to Avoid

There are times when an animatic will be the only feasible and affordable rough-production technique, such as when a celebrity won't do test ads or when expensive special effects are involved. Make certain that the illustrator is capable of work that's realistic, respectful, and as un-cartoonlike as possible. This may cost a bit more, but it's less expensive than getting burned by a misleading result.

---

2. How to test an ad in a way that approximates the real world

There are several methods of pre-testing advertising—some good, some not so good.

The worst by far is taking a couple of ads or storyboards into a focus group. Incredibly, this is done all the time. As noted, the best way to pre-test a campaign is with a reasonable facsimile, and a storyboard is simply an illustrated script that in no way represents a live commercial. Adding insult to injury is the focus group "method" itself. Six, eight or ten people sitting around a table "assessing" a storyboard or a print ad that's "read" by a moderator does not come close to the way that advertising is experienced in the real world. Many promising campaigns get killed in focus groups. Make sure yours doesn't.

Let's move to the serious methods of pre-testing advertising. There are five big, established advertising research firms: Millward Brown, ASI-Ipsos, ARS, DRI, McCollum-Spielman. Each has years of experience, a blue-chip client list, and "unassailable proof" that their methodology will predict an ad's marketplace impact. These methodologies are all well thought out, their similarities are greater than their differences, and depending on target audience, they can get expensive. (But for the savvy research director, there are now low-cost options. See the sidebar below.)

Each of these methods presents the test ad in its intended medium: a TV monitor, a magazine, and so forth. The environment is "cluttered" with other ads. The respondent is asked to recall the ad, play back its main points, and indicate whether the ad persuades them to take action. These answers are then compared to established norms. Diagnostic information is provided on important "qualitative" issues like likeability, credibility, confusion. These issues are probed via open-ended questions with the answers provided verbatim.

Brand name research versus DIY

If your management needs the security of big name research to validate advertising decisions, don't fight city hall. But the fact is, you can get quality research at a far lower cost by using one of the do–it–yourself services, like Survey Monkey, Zoomerang, Insight Express. Here's how they work: You write the questionnaire, the DIY outfit executes the study, you do the analytics. One question that invariably comes up is, What about norms? But it's an issue easily solved by including a competitive ad or two in the research. It means you'll be comparing your ad to it's real–world competition (for me a much better benchmark).

3. How to figure out what the test results really mean

As we know, and should always remember, *statistics is about probability, not about certainty.* The results from an advertising test should never be taken as the gospel, no matter how well the methodology approximates the real world. A careful reading of the results, and especially the verbatims, is always necessary. *There are no shortcuts.* Here, then, is a commonsense approach on how to determine probable winners, definite losers, and those in-between.

- **Probable Winners**—If the test ad scores significantly "above norm" for both recall and persuasion, and if a close reading of the verbatims indicates the target understood the message and liked the story, the odds are good that the test commercial will lead to a great campaign.

- **Definite Losers**—If the commercial gets scores poorly for recall and persuasion, and if the verbatim responses are unenthusiastic, then it's clear that the idea is not resonating with its target and should be dropped.

- **Those In Between**—The fact is, most test ads score "within the normative range." This should not be a death sentence. A "normative" score is arguably a good score. It's reasonable to assume that ads making it to the research phase have been carefully reviewed by "pros" who know what they're doing. That means the database from which these norms are calculated is based on quality data points. Here then is how to assess an ad that scores in the "normative range."
  - If the recall score is average or poor, but the motivation score solid and the verbatim responses

promising, then there's something to work with. The brand name might be obscured or part of the commercial might be hard to follow.

- If the commercial gets a good recall score, but it's not persuasive, and the verbatims are not promising, then the ad is being remembered for the wrong reasons, and the advertising idea should probably be dropped. (Had the Michael Jordan/Rayovac commercial mentioned earlier been evaluated this way, millions of dollars would likely have been saved.)

Hazards to Avoid

The temptation to run with the campaign that gets the best numbers can be irresistible, especially at big organizations where the score is the only thing upper management learns about. But high scores can mislead. A great song or a great actor can sometimes be so entertaining it improves all the metrics. That's why a close reading of the verbatims is so crucial. It's the best way to be sure the intended message was convincingly communicated. Sometimes it will mean the lower-scoring commercial is the better choice.

7 How to get a great test score, and still get a great ad

The big research services all "add value" with "lessons learned" from their many years of experience and thousands of commercials tested. They've put every conceivable "executional element" through the rigors of regression analysis to determine which improve and which diminish a commercial's impact. Many of the resulting "lessons" are excellent, well worth studying and applying.

But some of them are naïve, sometimes frustratingly so. That's what sometimes happens when a well-intentioned research analyst, who knows little about how a creative team works, writes the lesson. It's these misguided suggestions that often discredit what should otherwise be valuable insight into what exactly makes effective advertising effective.

Take, for instance, the common advice on how to improve a commercial's recall score: *Mention and show the brand within first 5 seconds, and then mention and show it a couple more times after that.* This obviously works, as an execution's recall score is a measure of how many respondents in the test panel recall the brand's name.

But a high recall score itself does not a successful campaign make. And to any creative director worthy of the title, the notion of opening up a TV commercial with the brand name is almost always limiting. It effectively kills off any buildup of suspense; it calls for the punch line before the setup; it even makes that most traditional of techniques, the problem/solution, a hard one to execute.

Here's how the research companies should rewrite their guidance on recall: The commercial that's highly memorable is one that typically tells a relevant and positive story with the brand as its hero. When the commercial introduces the brand, it does so clearly, prominently—ideally, said and seen—and with enough time for the brand to register.

> *We shot a 30-second commercial for BreathSavers that didn't introduce the brand until the twenty-third second, but it scored well above the norm for recall. The commercial featured a scruffy young guy floating on a raft for twenty days before being "rescued" by a drop-dead gorgeous girl partying on a luxury yacht. Her first comment to him was "Nice breath! BreathSavers?"*

Having studied the lessons the research services teach, and having spent many hours with copywriters, art directors, and producers—here are the best of these lessons rewritten to be helpful and actionable to anyone in the advertising development process:

What improves an ad's memorability?

1. The storyline must be relevant and easy to follow (*just like any good story*).
2. The brand must be presented clearly, prominently, and with plenty of time to register (*at what point it's presented matters less*).

3. Humor, when appropriate, works well; so does product news (*most people turn to the media for entertainment and for news*).

4. Kids, animals, and beautiful people have stopping power (*find out why in the sidebar below*).

5. Attractive, articulate "real people" can be intriguing (*why else would reality shows be so popular*).

6. Continuing characters can become effective brand surrogates (*this is a better way to get the multiple mentions the research companies recommend*).

What diminishes an ad's memorability?

7. Anything that's confusing or illogical or too subtle (*it stops the viewer as the rest of the ad rushes on*).

8. Too many copy points (*most of us can process only a few points at a time*).

9. Music or sound effects that compete with the copy (*seems obvious, but happens all the time*).

10. Moving too quickly off the brand (*remember, the name needs time to register*).

What improves an ad's persuasiveness?

11. A positive, upbeat, hopeful presentation (*does a negative sales rep ever sell?*).

12. A credible reason-to-believe the brand's promise will be kept (*consumers are smart; they require proof*).

13. A clear, positive, relevant comparison to another brand (*all the research services agree*).

What diminishes an ad's persuasiveness?

14. Condescension or whininess (*no one wants to hear it*).

15. Meaningless comparisons (*compare real issues, not the irrelevant; your customer won't be amused, or sold*).

Babies, Animals, Beautiful People, and Recall Scores

Why do we stop to look at babies, animals, and beautiful people? It has to do with evolutionary psychology. We're programmed to protect and nurture vulnerable babies. We take notice of animals, as they once threatened our daily existence. We gawk at beautiful people because we want to work with them, so to speak, to carry on the species. It's also why we see TV commercials that feature infants offering investment advice, ducks and lizards selling insurance, and Catherine Zeta-Jones hawking cell-phone service. Is the use of these well-worn techniques smart, or cynical, or lazy? Some would answer, "Never mind, they work."

8 Producing a full-up commercial—The five key issues

Forgive the clichés, but the full-up production of a TV campaign is where the "rubber meets the road" and ends up with a "moment of truth."

The first thing to understand is that full-up production is a complex process. The collection of talent brought together to produce a film that's rarely longer that 30 seconds is extraordinary: writers, artists, producers, directors, actors, composers, musicians, graphic designers, film editors, always lawyers, and sometimes trained animals. There could be fifty, seventy-five, a hundred people involved. Scores of issues must be examined and decided on. That it all gets done in a matter of weeks—sometimes brilliantly—never ceases to amaze, no matter how many times one has been through the process.

If you're the client on the line, what can you do to help facilitate the best possible outcome? Weighing in on each decision would be impossible. Attempting to would be counterproductive. But there are five big, important issues that a savvy client should pay special attention to: 1) the director, 2) the talent, 3) the pre-pro meeting, 4) the serendipity factor, and 5) the all-important first viewing.

The Director

There are three "quality" levels of director: 1) A-list directors, 2), B-list directors, and 3) young directors on the way up.

When times are good, A-list directors get to work whenever they want. They're very expensive, but very talented, and generally worth the money. If your media budget is $25 or $50 million, and a couple "A" directors are interested, it makes sense to go with one. A talented director can lift a campaign from good to great, and the great campaigns always pay back quickly.

But if the assignment calls for shooting a simple pool-out of a well-established campaign, a solid B-list director might do just fine.

As for "young directors on the way up," the time to consider one is when production money is limited. Make a good choice and the results can be terrific. But make sure there's extra time for your agency to find and then work with the right young director.

How to weigh in: Look carefully at the reels of the three directors the agency final bids. You should see examples of commercials that give you confidence these directors have good and relevant experience. If you feel strongly the work of one director better represents the brand's character, say so with conviction. If the agency feels otherwise, hear them out, and then make an informed decision.

The Talent

When Daryl Zanuck was casting for a young actress to play Scarlet O'Hara in *Gone With the Wind*, he auditioned hundreds of women and needed a full year and half before settling on Vivien Leigh. She was, as we all now know, a brilliant choice. Would the movie have been as compelling without her? It's difficult to see how.

The right talent is equally important to a great advertising campaign. But Madison Avenue is not Hollywood. When a casting call goes out for a new campaign, the talent must be chosen within a couple of weeks. That means auditions, callbacks, recommendations, client approval, contract signing—all in just two, three weeks.

How to weigh in: When you're rushing, and rushing is endemic to commercial production, even the pros sometimes misjudge and miscast. There's nothing like the sinking feeling you get when you arrive at the pre-pro meeting the day before the shoot and you're presented with talent you know is wrong. Better to be safe, as too much is on the line to be sorry. Insist on seeing candidates at least a week before the shoot, even if they're "not quite right." This will confirm that you, the agency, and the director are all on the same page—and if you're not, you'll have the time to regroup.

The Pre-Production Meeting

A savvy client of mine always came to the pre-production meeting, but never attended the shoot. She understood that the pre-pro is where the most important agreements are reached. She felt her presence at the shoot would not add, and might even detract. Most clients don't stay away, but they should know that for them the pre-production meeting is more important than the actual shoot.

How to weigh in: Assuming the talent has already been chosen, the most important part of the pre-pro meeting is the director's interpretation of the storyboard. Pay close attention. Make sure the director's vision jibes with yours. Sometimes the director will suggest an alternative scene. If it's an obvious improvement, and your agency agrees, go with it. But if you're not sure, don't be shy. Decisions made at pre-pro meetings are difficult to reverse. That said, remember the serendipity factor—it often shows up at the shoot. Encourage some experimentation, but make sure pre-pro agreements are absolutely kept.

The Serendipity Factor

We were producing a new campaign for Palmolive Dishwashing Detergent with the stars of a short-lived NBC sitcom called *The Mommies*. In the eleventh hour, ABC decided to reject the campaign because it took place in a kitchen just like the one in *The Mommies*, and therefore "promoted" a competitive network's program. But the director (he was young and "on the way up") desperately wanted the job, and came up with a clever overnight fix. He designed a cardboard set in a cartoon style. It was clearly a kitchen, but nothing at all like the Mommies' set. Our client loved it. ABC was trumped. And the campaign tested through the roof—with the cartoon set itself highly memorable. *The Mommies* went on to sell lots of Palmolive for the next six or seven years.

How to weigh in: Leveraging the serendipity factor is obviously tricky. How does one plan to take advantage of the unexpected? Here's one way: Tell your agency that you insist that the approved campaign must be faithfully shot and delivered. Also tell them that you expect each "production artist" involved in the project—the director, the editor, the special effects house—to look for opportunities to "plus" the campaign. Make sure they get a bit of leeway to perform their magic. And don't overload them with endless requests for myriad alternatives. As to deciding on which "plusses" actually improve the campaign, let your judgment, and the judgment of those you trust, be your guide.

The All-Important First Viewing

Actually, there are two important first viewings: the *rough-cut* viewing, and the *finished commercial* viewing.

Like its name suggests, the *rough cut* is the "uncorrected film" edited together into a rough commercial, with no or few editorial enhancements, like dissolves, special effects, titles, music, mixed sound, or corrected color. Once the rough cut is approved, these enhancements are added, and the *finished commercial* is presented.

How you view the commercial at these initial presentations is deceptively important. That's because the first time you see a commercial, you see something different than what the creative team sees. Here's why: They've been locked in an editing room for days. They've seen edits, re-edits, and more re-edits. The commercial is now imprinted on their brains. They anticipate the next scene before it appears. As a result, the commercial for them slows down. To compensate, they sometimes add scenes. Sometimes they add too many. When this happens, the commercial to the first time viewer seems rushed. I'll often say, "It's got too many cuts; it feels rushed." The producer invariably looks at me like I'm talking about a different commercial. But make no mistake: Your impression at this point is more representative of your customers' than the agency's creative team.

How to weigh in: Before you look at the rough or finished film, announce that you'll look at it one time only, and then comment. This will be greeted with gasps. Respond as follows: "This commercial is costing me hundreds of thousands to make and millions to air, and for that kind of money, I expect it to move product the first time it runs." When the agency says, "But a campaign builds over time," you say, "Great! A commercial that sells every time will build better over time." You'll probably look at the cut a couple of times, but your first viewing is the most important, and should weigh heavily as you make your comments.

How much should a commercial cost to produce?

This is a supercharged issue. There's widespread paranoia that advertising production costs are often much higher than they should be. There's even a cottage industry of cost consultants that feeds, and feeds on, this paranoia. But the fact is, I've never seen blatant or purposeful overcharging. Clearly some judgment goes into building a cost estimate, but if the three-bid system is rigorously employed, good value for the money should be delivered.

As to what drives the cost of a TV commercial up or down, the most consequential factor is the complexity of the creative concept.

- The commercial with multiple locations, many actors, plus computer animation could cost $1 million, even $2 million, especially if an A-list director is involved.
- But the commercial that features a talking head, shot by a solid B-list director on a simple set, might cost $250,000, maybe less.

Can it be done for less than that? The answer is a definite maybe. There are now many production tactics that in the right hands can save money without compromising impact. (See the sidebar below.)

Avatar versus *My Big Fat Greek Wedding*

According to the trades, *Big Fat Greek Wedding* cost $5 million to produce; *Avatar* cost ten times that, about $500 million. Both movies were highly successful. But, obviously, you don't have to spend a gazillion dollars to produce a great movie—nor does take a million to get an effective TV commercial.

But make no mistake: A great director, a great film editor, a great music director, a great graphics designer—can make a good idea better, and a great idea greater.

If, however, you're pressed for money, if the Great Recession has forced you to make do with less, especially when it comes to TV production, *it can be done*. Here's how: Before the campaign exploratory kicks off, tell your agency, in the clearest possible terms, that you've only got, let's say, $150,000 for production, and then request that they come back with ideas that cost no more than $150,000 to produce.

They'll likely to come back with simpler ideas that are easier to produce. And since simpler ideas are often better ideas, there's opportunity here for the occasional win-win. The *Greek Wedding* producers did it; so can you and your agency.

9 When to change ads

The sixth century BC storyteller Aesop is credited with the timeless maxim, "Familiarity breeds contempt." Its application to this issue is obvious. We should replace ads before they become too familiar and "wear out."

Now the hard part: Exactly how many times must an ad be seen, heard, or read before it becomes too familiar and wears out? It's an issue for which there is no shortage of theories, points of view, and formulas. As usual, the simplest and the most obvious is the best.

It comes to us via ARS, one of the big research houses. ARS has studied the effects of multiple exposures on the persuasive power of TV commercials. The research shows that a commercial is most persuasive the first time it's seen and that it loses impact with each successive viewing. By the time a commercial's exposure has reached 1,100 to 1,200 GRPs*, its *persuasive power* will

---

*One GRP represents one percent of the target audience. A full explanation can be found in Chapter 11.

have been reduced by 50 percent, as this graph from ARS illustrates:

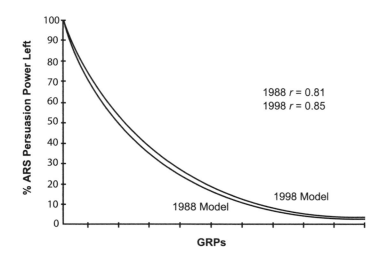

PRODUCTIVE ADVERTISING WEARS OUT (WORKS) QUICKLY IN A PREDICTABLE FASHION AS IT IS AIRED

1988 r = 0.81
1998 r = 0.85

1998 Model
1988 Model

% ARS Persuasion Power Left

GRPs

Source: Blair, M. H. "An Empirical Investigation of Advertising Wearin and Wearout." *Journal of Advertising Research* 27, 6 (1987): 45-50.

Let's now translate this technical media data into practical terms, easier to understand. A typical schedule of 1,100 to 1,200 GRPs will reach approximately 90 percent its target audience *on average* twelve or thirteen times. (Heavy viewers will see it more, light viewers less, but the "typical" viewer will see it about this many times.) What ARS is then telling us is that by the time the viewer sees the commercial twelve or thirteen times, its power to persuade will have diminished by half.

This makes sense. The first time a good ad is seen, it's new and different; after it's been seen thirteen times, it's familiar and less interesting—like any rerun.

To drive the point home, think about those times when the same ad runs over and over and over. It quickly becomes familiar, and it soon becomes annoying.

Anyone watching the Winter Olympics a couple years back could not help seeing a commercial for an Rx arthritis medicine starring Dorothy Hamill gliding pain-free across the ice to the strains of "It's a Beautiful Morning". It must have run every day of the Olympics, during every competition, sometimes three or four times an hour. Within a couple of days this upbeat commercial went from engaging to predictable to maddening—at least for me and my family.

Here, then, are a couple of practical and affordable guidelines on when to change TV commercials as well as ads in other media:

- **TV commercials** should be replaced after they've been seen an *average* of ten to fifteen times. Run a commercial more than that, and it's like paying good money to a sales rep who's become bored working the same territory too long.

- What about **print ads or radio commercials?** There's no definitive research, but since these ads are less complex than TV commercials, it's reasonable to assume they will wear out sooner. The suggestion here is that print ads and radio commercials not be exposed to their target more than ten times.

- As for **outdoor or transit ads**, they are generally used as "reminders" to keep brand awareness up while print or TV delivers the full story. Since these ads get seen with high frequency (every morning on the subway or bus, or on the highway to the office), out-of-home ads should not stay up longer than several months.

- Most **Internet ads** are essentially low-cost direct-response ads, and should therefore be replaced as soon as their click rates begin to fall.

An important related issue is, How many campaign executions to schedule at any given time? There's no good research on this, but common sense would suggest that if the media schedule is a heavy one—over 125 GRPs a week, for instance—then it makes sense to run a couple of ads. *Had our Dorothy Hamill example been accompanied by a couple of pool-mates featuring other middle-aged Olympians, the campaign would have been more effective and a lot less annoying.*

Hazards to Avoid

Many clients balk at high production budgets. They argue that they'd rather spend their money buying media. A worthy objective, but sometimes naively applied. Saving money by running fewer ads more frequently is penny wise and counter productive. Don't fall into this trap. Replace commercials once they are worn out, even if that means cutting your media budget to produce more ads. (And remember *Avatar* vs. *My Big Fat Greek Wedding*: A great campaign requires a great idea, not a great production budget.)

10 When to change campaigns

This is a much tougher question to answer. There is no foolproof formula. It's essentially a judgment call. But one thing for sure, an effective campaign is a hard thing to come by. Replacing one should be done reluctantly, after careful consideration, unless fate dictates otherwise. As to the special circumstances that make changing campaigns a good idea, here are three:

1. When the campaign's core idea stops pooling out

The "Little Guy" in the Cheer campaign eventually ran out of distinctly different side-by-side demonstrations. They all started to look the same—but that took eight years! American Express ran its "Do You Know Me?" campaign featuring accomplished but not-well-known people for a decade before the idea ran its course. Similarly, Apple's Mac ran its terrific "cool guy" versus "nerd" side-by-side campaign for three years. Here, too, the skits started to look the same and it was time to move on. As of this writing, the long-running

AFLAC duck campaign is still running, but the effort to keep the work fresh is starting to show. That usually means the end is in sight.

Hazards to Avoid

The gravest threat to a long-running campaign can be new people assigned to the brand. That's because even the most experienced among us are never totally immune to "not invented here" syndrome. In its most virulent form, it's a killer. So, unless you're expressly brought in to change campaigns, be careful about fixing what's not broke. If you do decide a new campaign might be in the brand's interest, make sure the new work soundly beats the current work in an objective test. Even then, ask yourself, and those you trust, if the new option is better than the current campaign.

---

2. When a continuing character becomes problematic or irrelevant

Dave Thomas, Wendy's founder and enormously successful pitchman, died an early and untimely death, and Wendy's advertising has never been quite the same. Madge the Manicurist demonstrated how Palmolive "softens hands while you do the dishes" for twenty-five years, well into her seventies, when she could no longer connect with a thirty-year-old. As for the Tiger Woods affair: some sponsors bailed out, others swore loyalty; but the fact is, he's lost his credibility, and, as of this writing, has appeared in no ads that I've seen.

Situations like these cannot be controlled—but they can be planned for. (See the hazards section below.)

Hazards to Avoid

The research services find that *continuing characters* can be highly effective, but as we've just seen, they carry some risk. To limit the risk, a backup campaign is a must. Backup campaigns used to be standard for most brands, but they're expensive to develop, and with markets changing so fast, they often become outdated before they see life. Nevertheless, if your campaign features a *continuing character*, you must have a ready backup, just in case the sky does happen to fall.

3. When the marketing environment changes

There are times when forces beyond our control alter the basic assumptions upon which a brand is built. This can be a treacherous time, for your brand and your campaign. Let's see how two brands handled change well and one that did not.

- **Bayer Aspirin** was dying a slow death as less-irritating analgesics like Tylenol and Advil were pioneered. But Bayer found (or lucked into) an alternative reason-for-being, and leveraged it to the hilt. Aspirin prevents blood from clotting, and blood clots are implicated in many heart attacks. That's why doctors recommend an aspirin a day for people at risk of coronary heart disease. Bayer understood the opportunity, and repositioned itself as a doctor-recommended way to help prevent heart attack. And with a new campaign, the brand rebuilt itself into a business bigger and more vital than ever.

- **Budweiser** ran advertising for much of the '70s and '80s that famously declared, "This Bud's For You!" It was all about success and celebration, and the role that a good beer can play. Then the microbreweries started popping up, and with their promise of better taste, began chipping away at big Bud. But the Busch crowd had the smarts and guts to do what must have been painful—they recognized the threat, came down off the mountain, refocused Bud's strategy, and launched a competitive and functional campaign. It preempted *freshness* and the superior taste a *fresh* beer delivers. To prove its *fresh* credentials, Bud literally dated its cans. This was no half measure. It took imagination and courage. More important, it worked.

- **Snackwell's** should have gone to school on Bud, but didn't, and paid a big price. In the mid-'90s, Snackwell's was a runaway hit as a low-fat, good-tasting line of snacks. But as the decade progressed, Americans became more sophisticated about fats, and fats per se became less worrisome. And the important "gap" that Snackwell's had been filling became less important. But unlike Bayer or Bud, the brand didn't respond strategically. They attempted a few new TV campaigns, but never offered a new reason why the brand should be reconsidered. Today, Snackwell's is a small promotional brand that Kraft is essentially milking.

Hazards to Avoid

Advertising alone rarely solves a basic marketing problem, but too many clients too often ask their agencies to do just that. And when the agency doesn't come through (how could they?), the agency often takes the hit. If your market changes, your marketing strategy must change, and then your creative strategy and campaign may or may not change. Don't put the cart before the horse; it will be tough on your agency and, eventually, tougher on you.

---

11 The elusive media threshold—How to find it

If you're in the business of building brands, *you probably cannot afford not to advertise.* That's because a product or service never becomes a brand *without high awareness.* And to keep the awareness of most brands effectively high, media support at or above the threshold level is always required.

> *Yes, it's true that Starbucks, with its high-traffic locations, doesn't need advertising to maintain high awareness, but try creating a new packaged coffee brand without at least threshold-level media support.*

This, of course, begs two questions: How does one locate the threshold level? and, What does it cost? Like so many advertising questions, the questions about media threshold generate all manner of responses. But, in this case, there is no one right answer. But there is a commonsense approach that can help most any brand locate its threshold level. (It's important to know this, because spending less, as you'll soon see, is like spending nothing—except it costs money.)

Let's start with a basic understanding of the nature of brand awareness. The dictionary defines awareness as "having knowledge of." We typically have knowledge of things that we consider important. Things that are not of urgent importance, like most brands, get pushed to the back of our minds. And without constant reminders, that's where they'll stay.

This is not speculation; it's backed up with solid proof. Let's begin with a review of a seminal study, quite old but still relevant, as it dramatizes just how perishable a commodity awareness can be. It's from *Effective Frequency*, a book by Michael Naples, the once and longtime Director of Research of Lever Brothers. Naples validates the obvious: When media support is abruptly stopped, awareness abruptly falls off; but when media support is consistent, awareness is not only maintained, it often improves.

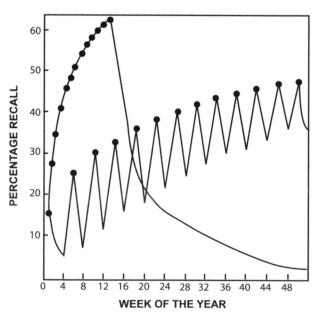

PERCENTAGES OF HOUSEWIVES WHO COULD REMEMBER ADVERTISING WEEKLY

With the benefits of consistent media support clearly established, the issue becomes: *What specific level of support is consistently required?*

Millward Brown, the big research house, has studied the issue and provides useful information. They reviewed scores of advertising tracking studies, and compared media support with the resulting awareness levels. The analysis found that most brands, generally—there are exceptions—require a schedule of at least 50 TV GRPs a week to maintain an adequate level of advertising awareness. (That advertising awareness drives brand awareness is obvious, so we'll take that small leap here.) Scheduling media weight below 50 GRPs resulted in awareness falling off; scheduling more that 50 GRPs typically caused awareness to rise. (If you don't know what a GRP is, see the best-ever definition below.)

Let's now put aside Millward Brown's 50 GRPs per week guidance for a moment, and consider another important lesson, again from Naples. He studied all the studies on "advertising frequency" and observed that, all things being equal, the target customer must be reached *a minimum of three times over a four-week period* before the campaign's message is "learned." This too seems altogether reasonable, as most of us need to see or hear a message a couple of times before it sinks in, especially if the message is not one of high urgency.

Good lessons both, but they become even more convincing when we put them together. Here's how: A weekly 50 GRP schedule that runs four weeks means 200 GRPs. According to Nielsen, a typical 200 GRP schedule reaches 60 to 65 percent of its audience about *three times*. So, what we have here is Millward Brown's 50 GRP finding in effect corroborating Naples's 3-frequency conclusion.

Let's go back to the original question: What level of media impact does a brand require in order to cross the threshold of effectiveness? The all-purpose answer is: When sufficient "weight" is scheduled to reach a majority of the brand's target audience at least three times every four weeks. For most brands, 50 GRPs per week is the threshold. Spending less or spending inconsistently will likely be a waste of resources and should be vigorously avoided.

But this is simply an approach. There's always room for judgment, and there are always exceptions. Here are three:

- If the brand is a seasonal one, like an allergy medicine, then brand awareness should be spiked in the spring, as pollen starts to swirl. It might make sense to schedule 125 or 150 GRPs in the first four or six weeks, before cutting back to a maintenance level.

- If your brand competes in a high-spend category, with the key players scheduling 150 or 200 GRPs per week, then 50 GRPs will not get your message heard above the competitive din.

- If you're launching a new product, and your intelligence indicates the competition's not far behind, you might determine that five or six frequency for the first three or six months is required to establish and insulate your business.

What is a GRP anyway?

One GRP, or one Gross Rating Point, represents one percent of your brand's target audience. For example, when the Super Bowl gets a 40 rating, that means 40 percent of your brand's target audience was watching the program. If you had ran two spots in the Super Bowl, this would have meant 80 GRPs.

GRPs are often expressed in terms of Reach and Frequency. When a typical media schedule delivers 900 GRPs, this means it *reaches* an estimated 90 percent of its target audience an average *frequency* of ten times (90 Reach × 10 Frequency = 900 GRPs).

GRPs are important because they represent a basic unit of media value. A *GRP* is to media what a *yard* is to cloth, an *acre* to land, a *byte* is to memory. And like the yard or the acre, the GRP is no more than a quantitative measure. Some acres are more fertile than others, and some GRPs are more impactful than others. More on this in chapter 12.

Now that we've set out an "approach" on how to locate the threshold spending level, let's move on to ten common-sense stratagems that will help get the best return on media investment.

12 Ten obvious (some only seem obscure) things to know about media planning and buying

The media function of the advertising business has become much more complex, and much more interesting. Twenty years ago media was a stepping-stone to account management. Today it's a career destination. Twenty years ago the big-three TV networks dominated. Today most households can choose from hundreds of channels. Twenty years ago there was no Internet. Today nearly 80 percent of homes are wired. Twenty years ago, you listened to radio via AM or FM. Today, you can listen via AM, FM, Internet, and satellite. And according to the Magazine Publishers Association, in 2009, despite the medium's troubles, 193 new magazines were launched!

How then to get the best return on your media investment in this rapidly changing environment? The answer is not all that sophisticated: Focus on fundamentals, use common sense, *and understand clearly what you're buying*.

But first, and most important, make sure that your campaign is an effective one. Nothing leverages a media investment more than filling the time and space with high-impact ads.

Second, make sure a couple of savvy media planners and tough negotiators are assigned to your business. If I were a client, I'd work at getting these people feeling good about me and my brand. The media sometimes bestow favors— like better positions, last-minute discounts, even free time they can't sell—and you want your media team feeling good about you when these favors get passed along.

Now on to ten obvious lessons, some of which had been stuck in obscurity:

1. **Build impact in your brand's best medium before adding a second or third.** Job One is to determine which medium is best at reaching your brand's target audience and delivering your campaign's message. Next, build a foundation that delivers at least 70 percent reach and three times frequency every four weeks over a substantial part of your brand's selling season. Then, and only then, consider adding a second medium. For many years, Motel Six scheduled just one medium, radio, but with a great campaign that featured a continuing character, Tom Bodett. Radio is the ideal medium to reach travelers looking for a good night's sleep at a good price. Radio was best for Motel Six, as skywriting might be for a sunscreen, as the fashion magazines might be for a new Italian designer. But for most successful mass-marketed brands…

2. **TV continues to be the fastest, and often the best, way to reach the most people, despite all the reports to the contrary.** Rarely does a day go by without an announcement in the trades about the demise of the TV commercial. Be careful, TV is arguably stronger than ever. Nielsen tells us that

TV viewing at the typical household has passed eight hours a day, dwarfing every other medium. And why not? The quality of TV programming gets better and better, and it's still, mostly, free. Suggestion: Never look at a media plan that doesn't include an exhibit that details cost per GRP and the four–week reach potential of all relevant media. You'll see that for most targets, even tech-savvy teens, TV is still the most efficient way to build the fastest reach. TV is one very strong medium, but the fact is, two are almost always better. . .

3. **The campaign delivered via multiple media delivers *a whole bigger than the sum of its parts.*** It's a concept called *the multiplier effect.* Millward Brown, Nielsen, and Ipsos have all published studies validating its existence. The concept holds that when a target customer gets the same message via a couple of different media, the odds go up that the message is retained and acted upon. So, if you've got the money, and can afford two or three media, your media plan will likely deliver a whole bigger than the sum of its parts.

4. **More GRPs, a more effective media plan *doesn't make.*** As we've seen, one Gross Rating Point, or GRP, represents 1 percent of the target audience. That's all. No more. A GRP reflects nothing quali- tative. Whether you buy a 15 second time slot or a 60; whether your ad appears in the front of the magazine or buried in the back; whether it's black-and-white or 4-color—the number of GRPs you purchase will be exactly the same. But there's obviously a big difference in price, quality and impact. Warning: Beware the media plan

recommended because it delivers the most GRPs. To be sure, GRPs are important, but by themselves, they tell about half the story. Informed judgment is invariably required to make good media decisions.

5. **If they can deliver the message, smaller media units generally beat larger ones.** The full-page magazine ad positioned next to editorial is more likely to get read than the twice-the-price two-page spread. That's because the reader of the article next to the ad *spends more time next to the ad*. As for TV, all the research services consistently find that 15-second commercials typically deliver 70 to 75 percent of the impact of 30s, even though they're half as long. It's because a shorter message is easier to remember. *The point is, you should always determine and schedule the smallest media unit capable of delivering your brand's full message.* Smaller units are obviously less expensive—and if the smaller ads are effective, your entire media program becomes substantially more efficient.

6. **Understand how much clutter you're buying into.** In the '90s, the average number of commercial minutes in primetime was 13; today it's up to 16 minutes. That might not seem like much, but 3 more minutes is 180 more seconds, and that means six more 30s, or twelve more 15s—and that is a lot. It's also why so many commercial breaks carry as many as eight to ten commercials. And there's no way the seventh or eighth commercial in a break can be as effective as the first or second. But the price of each is typically the same, because each represents the same number of GRPs, which, of course, is a misrepresentation of their value. The

same is true of magazines; some are stuffed with up to 300 pages of ads. Would you want your brand lost among the last 50? What to do? Make clutter a negotiating tactic. Demand that your ad is surrounded by less clutter, or is placed in an earlier position, or, better yet, demand both.

7. **Ads that run closer to the purchase date are obviously more effective, but obvious opportunities are too often missed.** For example, more people shop later in the week than earlier; the most shop on Saturday, the fewest on Sunday. If yours is a supermarket brand, it makes little sense to schedule ads on Sunday or Monday. However, most TV and radio stations sell Monday–Sunday or Monday–Friday schedules—this gives *them, the media*, considerable flexibility. Press your agency to press the media to schedule your ads on the days when your customer is most likely to be in the market. If the medium's not sold out, they might do it gratis. (If you're spending a lot, they definitely will.) Or they might charge a premium. But at least then you can make an objective evaluation.

8. **Don't overlook the most underrated medium.** Radio is probably the least glamorous among the many media. No one gets famous writing radio ads. No one wins big-time awards for radio ads. And they're hard to write; most are 60s, so they require about 150 to 175 words. That's a lot of writing. But for those willing to invest the time and energy—as the Motel Six agency did—radio can be powerful, and for good reason: The medium delivers the most captured of audiences. Think about it, most radio listening takes place in the

car: You can't leave the room, you're typically by yourself, you're not distracted, and you're relatively focused. All that, and radio time costs less to buy and the ads less to produce. So unless your brand requires a visual that can't be described well with words, it makes sense to give radio consideration.

9. **Since all media is highly perishable, eleventh-hour deals can be struck, if you're enterprising and disciplined.** A small company called Jeffrey Martin marketed niche products like Topol, The Smoker's Toothpaste. Much of their media was bought in the eleventh hour from radio and TV stations that would otherwise have been stuck with unsold inventory. They paid a small percentage of the rate-card price. Jeffrey Martin understood the obvious: If the time or space doesn't sell, the medium gets nothing, and something, anything, is better than nothing. How much of this Russian roulette you're willing to play depends on many things, but it seems to me that any steady advertiser would be smart to hold back some money and let the media know you'll pick up unsold inventory if it's deeply discounted. Unless we're in the midst of the Olympics, a presidential election, or a booming economy—there's always some time or space that doesn't get sold.

10. **As for product placement, a lot of coverage, but little proof, and questionable value, so proceed with caution.** Spielberg's *Minority Report* included brands that paid to be placed in the movie. He apparently didn't feel the placements compromised the movie's integrity. So this controversial tactic is here for now. A couple of concerns, and some advice:

- The whole notion of creating programming or movies with a secondary objective of selling goods and services is troublesome. The best entertainment is obviously entertainment first. Spielberg notwithstanding, even the most innocuous of product placements have some corrupting influence. (That most any kid can spot most any placement in about half a second says volumes.)

- Who then should consider product placement? The answer: Only a mega brand very well known to its target audience. And then only after a good job has been done in the brand's primary media. Just be careful the placement is not so painfully obvious that the audience gets a laugh or, worse, gets annoyed.

- What to pay for product placements is a genuine conundrum. When you buy 3,000 GRPs for a new product, you get 50 percent awareness. But what do you get when you buy a product placement? You basically get a brand name reminder. What's the reminder worth? If it's up for 5 seconds, is it worth 16.67 percent of a 30 second commercial? If Jennifer Aniston is drinking it, is it worth more. Tough questions with no clear answer. The advice here is don't bother unless your budget is so large you can afford to take a shot on a tactic yet to prove its effectiveness.

What about the Internet as an advertising medium? As we noted upfront, online advertising has become very important, so much so it's deserving of its own chapter.

13

Internet Advertising— Still a work in progress, but it works, some of it very well

In the first edition of Shortcuts I hesitated to identify "lessons learned" as the Internet was still reeling from the bursting of its bubble. To be sure, the new medium represented exciting potential, but it was less obvious back then which strategies and tactics could be depended on to consistently deliver a positive return.

That has clearly changed. No matter what kind of business you're in, no matter where your business gets done, *a digital strategy is now a must.* And there's now substantial evidence several strategies can be confidently employed to profitable effect.

Let's take a closer look, and to help us, let's follow the money. The money getting allocated to Internet advertising has been growing at rapid speed. It will pass $25 billion in 2010. That puts Internet spending ahead of Magazines, ahead of Radio, and soon to be ahead of Newspapers.

The most important driver of this growth has been the extraordinary effectiveness of search engine marketing (SEM). Nothing epitomizes that effectiveness more than Google. It's now the world's tenth most valuable company, bigger than P&G, IBM, GE, and AT&T. The heart of Google's business is its search engine, and the high likelihood of payback SEM represents. It's no surprise that nearly half of all online spending goes to search:

Online Advertising in 2010

Type	$MM	%
Search	12,374	49.3
Banner Ads	5,477	21.8
Classifieds	1,958	7.8
Rich Media	1,576	6.3
Lead Generation	1,531	6.1
Video	1,506	6.0
Sponsorship	402	1.6
Email	276	1.1
Total	**$25,100**	**100%**

Source: eMarketer 2010

But what is also obvious, or should be, is that for SEM to be effective, the website at the end of the search must be effective as well. It's a two-part equation. Let's focus on the website part first.

What are the key characteristics of the most successful websites?

The best way to answer this question is to visit several heavily trafficked websites and study them. And the best way to do that is by assuming the mindset of the first time visitor, and following in her footsteps:

First, she decides to satisfy a specific information need;

second, she goes to her PC, iPad or smart phone;

third, she visits her favorite search engine;

fourth, types in a relevant keyword or a phrase;

fifth, spots a promising "organic" or "sponsored" link;

sixth, she clicks on the link; and

seventh, arrives at the site expecting her information need to be satisfied.

"Search" is obviously very efficient, but it still takes some work, as many as seven steps to get to a website. When the visitor arrives, she's in no mood to do more work. That means your website must deliver—quickly. Here then are four facilitating characteristics she'll find at the Internet's best websites:

- **The information she's searching for is easy to spot, if not the first thing she sees.** Check: Geek Squad, Amazon, WebMB, KraftRecipes, Flickr—no effort is required at these sites to understand what's in front of you, and what to do next.

- **The language is crystal clear and easy to understand.** Check any inside Google page—the language is always lucid, easy to follow, fun to read.

- **The content is comprehensive and well organized.** Check Craigslist and WebMB—two very different sites, both loaded with information, but each, in its own way, well organized and easy to work with.

- **And compelling reasons are provided for her to make frequent return visits.** Check KraftRecipes. com and Tide.com—both provide practical advice and good ideas on how to make family life a little tastier, a little more convenient, a little less expensive; and both include easy registration for a smart, friendly newsletter.

Hazards to Avoid

It's important to remember that a website is not advertising. Advertising must first break through clutter, then convince its target to do something. Your website is different; it's a destination. The visitor has already decided to go there. Her attention is already focused. This means your website needs no drama; it breaks through no clutter. But too many in the website creation business push their clients to add "cool stuff." Be careful. If the "cool" addition does not facilitate a better experience, then it detracts. Nothing brings this home better than Craigslist. It's a well-organized classified. That's it. You'll find nothing there that's remotely cool. But Craigslist profits were estimated to hit $100 million in 2010. Now that's…cool!

How to drive qualified customers to your website?

There are many drive-to-site tactics, but most of the action is with SEM and banner advertising, where seven of ten Internet media dollars get spent. This is where we'll focus. As for the remaining tactics, there's not yet sufficient marketplace experience from which to draw firm conclusions. I'll deal with this in a future edition, or on my blog (check: ShortcutsToTheObvious.com).

Search Engine Marketing (SEM)—If your website is key to your business, SEM is a must. It's an extraordinarily efficient way to connect with interested customers. As a result, the odds that an SEM investment will deliver a positive return are comparatively high.

What's more, the cost of testing your way into an optimal program is very low. You can start by spending as little as $100 a day to figure out the most effective keywords and the best ad copy. You'll get daily results per keyword and per ad, and you can quickly change keywords and revise copy until you're getting the most hits for the least cost.

But for the best advice, check the how-to sections at the major SEM providers, especially Google—it's clear and practical and it works. (I've sold many books taking this advice.)

Banner and Display Ads—As a pure ROI play, these ads are getting harder to make work. Banner ad click-thru rates (CTR) have plummeted, now averaging less that 2 tenths of 1 percent. That's 1 click for every 500 impressions.

But with over 20 percent of Internet ad spending going to banner ads, they must be working for some marketers. Here's why: Most people don't casually visit websites; they go there with special needs; and if a well-constructed banner ad clearly addresses their special need, the results should be better.

For example, no one visits the section of the Mayo Clinic website devoted to ischemic stroke without special interest in the subject. So a display ad about an FDA-approved Rx medicine clinically proven to prevent debilitating stroke among high-risk patients should deliver a CTR substantially better than the dismal averages.

As for the design of an effective banner or display ad, a recent study from the research firm Dynamic Logic examined the best and least effective ads. It includes several commonsense recommendations:

- *Intrigue is rarely a good strategy in online campaigns. Get right to the point, because you can't expect the user to wait around and watch the ad in its entirety.*
- *The size of the ad counts less; the relevancy of the message and the clarity with which it's delivered, counts much more.*

Good advice for any medium, especially one that's built for speed.

How the Internet helps build brands that would never have had a chance

Is there anything more commodity-like than flour? It's a bland and basic recipe ingredient. There's little difference among the flour options on the shelves. But King Arthur Flour managed, remarkably, to transform itself into a strong brand with a loyal following. Visit its website and sign up for its newsletter and you'll soon understand why. It's all about wonderful recipes, deliciously presented. The point is, this would not have been possible before the Internet. That's because to deliver the same experience, King Arthur would have needed print advertising and glossy catalogues. That would have triggered media, mail, and paper costs. The price premium required to support these expenses would have been far too high for any sensible homemaker to pay. But with the Internet, these costs are small or nil, so great brands, like King Arthur flour, are being created that would never have had a chance.

---

14 How to get better campaign integration, less painfully

Twenty years ago the phrase *campaign* integration would have been met with, "Huh?" It had not yet become part of advertising's vocabulary. Ad agencies back then worked mostly in mass media—TV, radio, print, out-of-home. When a creative team produced a campaign, it was executed in some or all of these media. Each ad—whether TV, radio, or billboard—reflected the same creative strategy, the same campaign idea, and many of the same campaign hallmarks. In other words, *a campaign was not a campaign unless it was integrated.* Why then has this ostensible redundancy become so important?

In the 1990s, direct marketing, database marketing, and digital marketing became less mysterious, more understandable, and more effective—so much so that marketers across the spectrum began to build these one-to-one disciplines into their plans. But they're substantially different than their mass-media cousins. The experience and skill set required to design a website or an SEM program is substantially different than that required to art direct a TV commercial or an out-of-home campaign.

One consequence is the need to now have three or four different creative teams, often at competing agencies, working together to execute one campaign. That these collaborations work well is obviously important, but much too often, they become exercises in exasperation. Remember, nothing motivates the best creative teams more than the opportunity to create original advertising. But in this new world, *some creative teams are told to put their creativity on hold and produce executions based on someone else's idea.*

And despite all the assurances from the big agencies and their holding companies that their many different units work together happily and seamlessly—and how they integrate just as seamlessly with units at competing agencies—*the cold hard truth is that the best creative teams have little interest in executing someone else's campaign.* This should be obvious. To think otherwise is to be naïve.

So when the direct or digital team shows up with work that doesn't quite represent the core campaign, it's not because they don't know how to do it, it's because they hate doing it. Remember, it's in their DNA to be original.

All that said, if you manage a brand with a campaign that includes mass and direct media, *seamless integration* should be high on your agenda. A real campaign—one that travels well across media and borders—is always more effective and less costly. (There's never a good reason why the photo in the print ad shouldn't be used in the fulfillment piece. Nor is there any serious rationale why a great campaign for a global brand developed in Brazil or New Zealand can't run in North America.)

How then to mitigate the problem? (*To mitigate* is the best one can hope for; *to solve* would be an exercise in futility.)

1. Top clients should regularly express their sympathetic understanding that no one gets into advertising to execute someone else's campaign. But they should be equally emphatic about their certainty that the most effective campaigns are seamlessly integrated, strategically and executionally. Acknowledging both truths side by side will go a long way toward building the respect and trust so necessary for these fragile relationshipsto work reasonably well.

2. When a new campaign is developed, the lead creative team must get buy-in from the direct and digital teams. This will accomplish three things:
   - It will expose any inherent problem executing the campaign in the content media;
   - it will go a long way toward building a sense of partnership among the creative teams; and
   - it will facilitate the reality that they who create the core campaign must also serve as its "keeper." In other words, the lead creative team should review all the major work, regardless of discipline, before it goes forward. The importance and difficulty of this task should not be underestimated, but it's got to be done.

3. Whether the various "disciplines" are all located at one agency or at competitive agencies, the extended team should meet regularly. Once a month is ideal. At these meetings the client should review business results, campaign results, and strategic priorities. The agencies should show and tell what they've been up to. Everyone there should look for ways and means to save time and resources.

4. But after all is said and done, clients pay good money for campaign integration and expect that

it's a subject taken seriously, despite anyone's agenda to the contrary. One final way to make sure your brand gets the integration it deserves is to make *seamless integration* a money issue in an incentive compensation arrangement. More on this in the next chapter.

15 How to get the best from your agency, and what to pay for it

First, understand Pareto's Principle. "A minority of causes, inputs, or effort usually lead to a majority of the results, outputs, or rewards." In other words, the 80/20 rule.

Here's the point: Whether yours is a global brand at a publicly traded holding company or a regional product at a small local shop, it's never more than a few people who make the real difference. That's because the core campaign we've talked so much about is always the creation of a talented and motivated creative team—often no more than a creative director, art director, copywriter, and producer. And since the campaign is the real leverage in this business, it's crucial to get the right creative people assigned and dedicated to you and your business.

How to make that happen? A couple of ways: First, and always, understand and embrace the fact that nothing drives a talented creative team more than the prospect of doing original work. A*nd the best means toward that end, as we've seen, is a focused and differentiating creative brief.*

It also makes good sense to get know your creative team. Invite them to lunch, take them to your sales meetings, call them directly, reward them for good work. In other words, make them your partners.

> *Colgate-Palmolive went so far as to create a phantom stock program for important agency people dedicated to their business. Every year they were awarded several shares, so they had a direct interest in their client's success. The program ultimately ran into regulatory problems and was discontinued, but Colgate-Palmolive clearly understood the difference the right agency partners could make to their business.*

Next, pay your agency fairly. The rub, of course, is what exactly is fair. Some would argue that fair is simply what the market will bear. Many clients approach the issue just this way, and shop for the best price every couple of years.

But savvy marketers understand that "buying" advertising is not like buying petroleum or memory or drill bits, where you generally pay for what you get. With advertising, you rarely pay for what you get—you get more, or you get less, depending on the effectiveness of the campaign. A superior campaign turns a $20 million investment into $25 million, maybe $30 million in impact. The creative that's wanting has the opposite effect.

It follows then that the agency producing the campaign that delivers the higher return deserves higher compensation. The best compensation models do just that. To be sure, there are many agency compensation models. Here's a good one: a two-step approach that rewards great work, encourages efficiency, and is easy to understand and administer.

Step One: Tightly estimate the cost of running the account. This is best done by the client and agency first agreeing on a scope of work—the specific projects the agency will work on during the year. Next, the agency develops a cost estimate based on the level of staff and the number of hours required to get the work done. Two tactics to consider:

> **First,** it's always easier for a client to cut its ad budget than for an agency to reassign dedicated people. And when people are reassigned, it's hard to get them back when budgets are reinstated. Here's what more clients are doing: They'll guarantee 80 percent of the full-year cost estimate with the proviso that key people will remain available to them.

> **Second,** these estimates are just that, inexact estimates. But there's an elegant way to have them encourage efficiency. Simply agree that agency labor costs be adjusted only when they're over or under estimate by 10 percent or more. This incentivizes the agency to work efficiently. If they work at 97 percent of estimate, they keep 3 points; if they work at 108 percent, they lose 8 points.

Hazards to Avoid

Agency people are notoriously bad at filling out time sheets. Back in the media commission days they never had to, and they've yet to get the hang of it. Tell your agency that you expect time sheets to be filled out promptly by everyone on your account, and that your auditors will occasionally show up unannounced to double check. Remember what Reagan said when he was negotiating arms reduction with Gorbachev: "Trust, but verify." Good advice when it comes to agency time sheets.

Step Two: Tie the agency's profit to the agency's performance. The argument over how to measure agency performance has raged from time immemorial. Rather than a rehash, here is a practical model that anyone can work with. It calls for awarding "markup" points in three broad performance criteria. The award points are then added up, and agency's labor costs marked up by a percentage equal to the award point total.

Here are examples of the types of criteria against which to evaluate an agency's performance:

1. **Pre-Launch Results:** Included here should be *objective* factors like strategic concept test results that led to a validated strategy and/or the advertising test scores achieved by the launch campaign.

2. **Post-Launch Results:** This too should be based on *objective* criteria such as marketplace results and/or awareness levels and/or response rates or some combination of such criteria.

3. **Agency Team Performance:** Evaluation of the team's performance should be always included, with both objective and *subjective* criteria. Were they always responsive? Were cost estimates always accurate? Did they bring forward new ideas, or simply do what was requested? Did they integrate seamlessly or reluctantly? Did the dedicated team remain that way, or was there turnover?

As for the "markup" points, award them as follows:

- 0 points for performance *below expectations*
- 7 points for *meeting expectations*
- 14 points for *beating expectations*
- 21 points for *beating expectations by an extraordinary margin*

Here are three hypothetical examples to illustrate how the system works:

1. If the agency *meets expectations* on each of the three criteria, the markup will be 21 percent (7 + 7 + 7). This yields a 17 percent profit margin, a bit below what most agencies hope for, but a solid return for sure. If the account's labor costs were $2 million, the agency's revenue would be marked up to $2.42 million, with $420,000 in profits.

2. If the agency delivers an *extraordinary* performance on two criteria and *beat* expectations on one, labor costs are marked up 56 percent (21+21+14), which yields a 36 percent profit. Marking up the same $2 million in labor cost results in $3.1 million in revenue and $1.1 million in profit—a huge return for an agency, but a small price for a terrific performance.

3. On the other end of the spectrum, the agency that gets zero or just 7 points is clearly in hot water, and should probably expect to be put on notice.

The essential point, once again, is this: A great advertising campaign always returns many more times its cost; it's why advertising agencies should always get paid extra when produce great campaigns, and docked when their work is wanting.

16 About the author and the blog

About the author

Mel Sokotch is a thirty-year veteran of three major advertising agencies: Ted Bates, Grey, Foote Cone & Belding (now DraftFCB). Among the national accounts he's led are Kraft, Colgate-Palmolive, Campbell Soup, M&M/Mars, Pfizer, GSK, Eli Lilly, Amgen, Merck, and Boehringer-Ingelheim.

Mel left the corporate world in 2005 to finish writing *Shortcuts to the Obvious*, which was first published in 2006. But with the advertising business changing rapidly, and with his experience broadening, especially as a consultant working directly with clients, the time was right for a substantial rewrite, hence this second edition.

In addition to writing, Mel regularly consults with agencies, clients and media companies. He's conducted seminars on positioning, on how to launch "later" to market brands, on how to apply FDA regulations regarding direct-to-consumer Rx medicine advertising, and on "great lessons from the great recession." He's written numerous articles, and is a frequent speaker at industry events.

Mel lives in New York City. His wife Joan is a local school administrator; son Jon is an attorney; daughter Amy, like her dad, is in advertising.

Mel can be reached via "contact" at www.ShortcutsToThe Obvious.com

About the blog

Mel's blog focuses on three issues: the importance of effective positioning, insights into what makes successful advertising successful, and how to save money without sacrificing quality. Like the book, blog posts are always short, and always based on real-world experience. Sign up at www.Shortcuts ToTheObvious.com.

INDEX

Not invented here syndrome,
66
NYC Marathon, 30

O

Online testing for strategic
concept statements, 33,
96
Oreo cookies, 23, 32, 38
Outdoor ads, when to
change, 63
Out-of-home advertising, 4,
63, 89

P

Palmolive Dishwashing
Detergent, 56, 66
Pareto's Principle, 93–94
Pepsi, 3, 30
Performance criteria, for
agencies, 96–97
Persuasion
diminishing, 52
improving, 51
reduction of, GRP formula
and, 61–62
of test-ad respondents, 46,
47
Photo-matics, for test ads, 43
Positioning
definition of, 10
importance of, 3–4
vs. positioning statement,
10, 18–20
using, 20
Positioning statement
definition of, 10
effective, building, 14–17
emotional payoff in, 13
examples of, 11–13
hazards to avoid, 17
issues addressed by, 10–13
vs. positioning, 10, 18–20
summary of, 10
using, 17–18
Pre-production meeting,
55–56
Pre-testing. See Test ads
Print advertising
creative exploratory and,
39
test ads for, 42, 44
when to change, 63
Problem/solution format, 50
Product placement, in
movies/TV, 80–81
Product positioning. See
Positioning

Products
becoming brands, 69
break-through, 7
See also Brands
Promises
benefit ladder and, 29
facts or insights used in,
27–28
hazards to avoid, 29, 31
higher-order benefits and,
29
to motivate target cus-
tomers, 28–29
See also Believability of
promises

Q

Qualitative issues, 45
Quantitative testing, 15–17

R

Radio advertising
captive audience for, 79–80
cost of, 80
creative exploratory and,
39
Motel 6 ads, 76
power of, 79–80
scheduling, 79
spending on, compared to
other media, 4
test ads for, 42
when to change, 63
Rayovac, 31, 47
Reach, of advertisements,
61–62, 73
Reagan, Ronald, 95
Recall, of test-ad respondents, 45–47, 49–50, 52
Relationships, in campaign
integration, 91
Reminders ads, 63, 81
Research
on banners or display ads,
87–88
brand name vs. do-it-yourself, 45
on continuing characters, 67
false positives/negatives,
42
firms, 44–45
inaccuracies in, 41
lessons learned from, 49,
50
on media support levels,
70–71
on media units and, 78
money, distribution of, 42

online services, 8
quantitative testing,
15–17
reliable, 42
on when to change ads,
63–64
See also Test ads
Return on investment (ROI),
73, 75, 87
Rip-o-matics, for test ads, 43
Rolaids, 30
Rough-cut viewing, 57–58
Rough-production technique,
44

S

Saab, 30
Satellite radio advertising,
spending, 4
Satellite TV advertising,
spending, 4
Seamless campaign integra-
tion, 90–92
Search engine marketing
(SEM), 83–84, 86–87
Seasonal brands, awareness
of, 72
Secondary points, 31, 81
Serendipity factor, 53, 56–57
Skill sets for today's cam-
paigns, 89
SlimFast, 29
Snackwells, 68
Snickers, 30
Southwest Airlines, 8, 9–10,
11–13, 17–18, 23
Spending threshold. See
Media spending
threshold
Spielberg, Steven, 80, 81
Starbucks, 69
Storyboards, 39, 44, 56
Strategic concept statements,
33, 96
Strategic concept test results,
96
Strategic Planner, 34
Super Bowl, 72
Survey Monkey, 45
Survey research, believability
of promises and, 30

T

Talent for advertising campaign, 54–55
Target customers
advertising as motivation
of, 28–29

best medium to reach,
  choosing, 76
brand awareness and, 6
GRPs representing, 61–62,
  71–73, 77–78
identifying in creative brief,
  24–25
positioning statements
  and, 11, 14
promises that motivate, 28
Technology for today's campaigns, 28–29
Television advertising. *See* TV
  advertising
Test ads
  bad, 46–47
  cost of, 42, 43, 44, 45
  finished ads represented
    by, 42–44
  full campaign, presenta-
    tion of, 39
  good, 46
  hazards to avoid, 47
  methods of, 44–45
  norms in, 45, 46
  pre-testing in focus groups,
    41, 44–45
  production techniques,
    43–44
  real world approximated
    with, 44–45
  roughs for, creation and
    testing, 40, 44
  scores, 46–47
  strategic concept state-
    ments and, 33
  See also Research
Third-party endorsements, 30
Thomas, Dave, 66

Threshold level. *See* Media
  spending threshold
Tide Stain Release, 24, 27,
  29, 32
Time sheets, 95
Topol Toothpaste, 3, 80
Transit ads, when to change,
  63
TV advertising
  clutter in, 78–79
  costs, 58
  15-second commercials,
    77–78
  memorable, 50–51, 56
  as primary medium, 3, 39,
    77
  production budgets and,
    64
  product placement in,
    80–81
  recall score and, 45–47,
    49–50, 52
  scheduling, 79
  spending on, compared to
    other media, 4
  talent for, 54–55
  testing, 42–43
  30-second commercials,
    50, 81
  when to change ads, 61–64
  when to change cam-
    paigns, 65–69
  See also Full-up commercial
Tylenol, 30, 67

U
Unique facts, believability of
  promises and, 30
United Airlines, 32

V
Verbatims, in test ads
  close reading of, 17, 46, 47
  interpreting test results
    and, 46–47
  open-ended questions
    and, 17, 45
  positioning statement and,
    17
  for qualitative issues, 45
Viagra, 3, 25, 26, 27, 31
Visa, 26, 29–30, 33–34
Visine Eye Drops, 31

W
WebMD, 85
Website
  vs. advertising, 86
  banners, 87–88
  click-thru rates, 87
  display ads, 87–88
  drive-to-site tactics, 86–88
  successful, characteristics
    of, 84–86
  See also Internet advertising
Wendy's, 66
Wilde, Oscar, 26
Williamsburg, VA, 7
Writers of creative brief, 34

Y
Yamamoto, Isoroku, 26
Yellow page advertising,
  spending, 4

Z
Zipcar, 26, 27
Zoomerang, 45
Zyrtec, 28